WRITING UP RESEARCH

Experimental Research Report Writing

for Students of English

Robert Weissberg and Suzanne Buker

Prentice Hall Regents   Englewood Cliffs, NJ 07632

To Sarah and Matthew
and
to the many international students,
past and present,
whose research interests enrich our
knowledge and our lives

Editorial/production supervision and interior design: Louisa B. Hellegers
Cover design: Photo Plus Art
Manufacturing buyer: Ray Keating

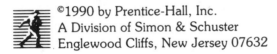©1990 by Prentice-Hall, Inc.
A Division of Simon & Schuster
Englewood Cliffs, New Jersey 07632

Printed in the United States of America

10 9 8

ISBN   0-13-970831-6

Prentice-Hall International (UK) Limited, *London*
Prentice-Hall of Australia Pty. Limited, *Sydney*
Prentice-Hall Canada Inc., *Toronto*
Prentice-Hall Hispanoamericana, S.A., *Mexico*
Prentice-Hall of India Private Limited, *New Delhi*
Prentice-Hall of Japan, Inc., *Tokyo*
Prentice-Hall of Southeast Asia Pte. Ltd., *Singapore*
Editora Prentice-Hall do Brasil, Ltda., *Rio de Janeiro*

CONTENTS

PREFACE

Writing Up Research is designed for high-intermediate and advanced ESL/EFL university students at the upper division or graduate level who are preparing to engage in scientific research in a variety of academic disciplines. For these students, the ability to write up the results of their own research in the form of technical reports, theses, dissertations, and even journal articles for publication is a key to their success as university students and as professionals in their own disciplines. Based on almost two decades of research in written English for science and technology, this book provides instruction and practice in this special area of academic writing.

The English of an experimental research report is highly conventionalized, a fact that represents a great advantage for non-native speakers as well as for their language instructors. If one can master the conventions, one can replicate the genre in an acceptable form. Moreover, the conventions are fairly consistent across a wide variety of scientific disciplines. They involve (1) structuring arguments and (2) matching linguistic forms to rhetorical purposes. This involves the writer's having to make a series of language choices. This text helps students to see what those choices are and to select the most appropriate—that is, the most conventional—option.

Although this book deals with technical English, the instructional language is not technical. It is accessible to high-level students regardless of their fields of study. The book does, however, contain many authentic examples of technical English taken from published experimental research reports in various fields. These show students how researchers actually use the conventions presented here in reporting on their work.

The best way for students to develop skills in writing the English of experimental research reports is to acquire them in a natural setting. This involves familiarizing themselves with published literature in their fields, conducting research projects with co-workers, and finally writing up their results. A textbook alone cannot substitute for this immersion environment; however, it can serve as a friendly and useful guide for students who are or will soon be involved in writing up their research.

ACKNOWLEDGMENTS

We wish to express our gratitude to the many workers in the field of English for science and technology whose research has provided the basis for this text. Principal among them are Louis Trimble, Mary Todd-Trimble, John Lackstrom, Robert Vly-Broman, and Larry Selinker, whose publications beginning in the 1970s first provided us with a rational approach to teaching the experimental research report. Of specific help in analyzing particular features of the report has been the work of John Swales on article introductions, Gregory West and Betty Lou Dubois on the discussion section, and Edward Cremmins on abstracts. Of course, we assume full responsibility for all rhetorical and grammatical analyses that appear here. We are especially grateful to Louisa Hellegers, our production editor at Prentice Hall, for her patience and careful attention to detail during the preparation of the book.

TO THE TEACHER

Writing Up Research may be used in academic English classes with students who are already enrolled in a university program or who are preparing for university entrance. The text can be used as part of a larger course in academic writing or it can be used throughout an entire semester. The language and content of the book are aimed at students with a TOEFL score of approximately 475 or higher. The material is appropriate for students planning to conduct research projects in the social sciences (including education), the natural and physical sciences, and engineering.

It is not the intention of this book to teach the research process itself. We assume that students will take courses in research methods and statistical analysis as part of their advanced studies or that they may already have this background. Our purpose is to show students how to translate their research activities into written reports that conform to the expectations of the English-speaking scientific/academic community.

Because most of the text models and many of the exercises used throughout *Writing Up Research* are based on excerpts from published experimental research reports, some of the terminology encountered will be new for students unfamiliar with particular fields of study. However, we have chosen these models on the basis of general interest level and accessibility to all research-oriented students. Additionally, we have attempted to represent as many different fields of study as possible in the excerpts. Students should be advised that they need not be familiar with every word in every model or exercise in order to recognize the conventions being studied or to understand the instructional point being presented.

An Instructor's Guide is available. It includes lesson suggestions for each chapter as well as answer keys to the exercises. It also includes notes on variations found across disciplines for some of the conventions covered in the text.

Finally, we hope that this book adequately fills an important need for you and your students: a straightforward and readable guide to the conventions English-speaking researchers follow when they write up their work.

TO THE STUDENT

This book is designed to help you learn to use the most important features of technical and scientific English in writing about research in your field. The principal type of writing treated here is the *experimental research report*, but the information in this book is also relevant to writing research proposals, literature reviews, summaries, abstracts, and especially theses and dissertations.

Many of the expressions and grammatical structures presented in these chapters may not be new to you. What will be new are the specific uses of these items in technical writing. These uses are called "conventions" because they are commonly followed by authors in most fields of research. Technical writing in English is very conventional. That is, when you have learned the conventions presented in this book, you will be able to write an acceptable report about almost any research project that you may carry out.

Examples from published research articles in various field are included in each chapter. These show you how scientists use the language forms you are studying when they write up their research. Sometimes these examples will include technical vocabulary that is new to you. Try not to be distracted by these terms; they should not interfere with your ability to understand the examples or to appreciate the way these writers use the language conventions you are studying. We hope, in fact, that you will find these excerpts to be interesting examples of research in many different fields.

In working through this book, you will be asked to find examples of published research in your area of interest. This is done because we believe that the more you read, the better you will write. You will also be asked to carry out an original research project to put into practice the conventions you are studying. Through these activities of reading, writing, and research practice, you will soon master the language of the experimental research report.

Robert Weissberg and Suzanne Buker
New Mexico State University

1

THE EXPERIMENTAL RESEARCH REPORT

OVERVIEW

An **experimental research report** is a paper written by an investigator to describe a research study that he or she has completed. The purpose of the report is to explain to others in the field what the objectives, methods, and findings of the study were. The report may be published in a professional *journal*, it may appear as a *monograph* distributed by a research institution or publishing company, or it may be written in the form of a *thesis* or *dissertation* as part of the requirements for a university degree.

We use the term "experimental research" here in a very broad sense, referring to various kinds of studies. One typical kind is the *controlled scientific experiment*, where the researchers conduct empirical tests while identifying and controlling as many factors as possible that may affect the outcome of the study. Another common kind of research is *correlational*, in which the investigators compare two or more different variables to determine if any predictable relationships exist among them. Other kinds of studies may deal with information obtained from *survey questionnaires* or from *case studies*. Still other studies use *computer-generated models* that attempt to explain or predict phenomena observed in the laboratory or in nature.

All these kinds of studies share some common characteristics. First, they are designed around a *research question*. As a possible answer to the research question, the researcher formulates a *hypothesis* and then designs the study in such a way as to reject or support the hypothesis. Also, such studies are usually *quantitative* — that is, they deal with numerical data obtained in carrying out the study. These data are usually treated with one or more *statistical tests* to determine how seriously the results should be taken.

The reports written to describe these different kinds of studies also have much in common. Normally, a report includes descriptions of the purpose, method, and results of the study. Complete results are usually presented in tables and graphs. Such a report contains references to other published works in the same area of study. A bibliography (a list of references) listing these works, along with all the information needed to find them in a library, is always included at the end of the report. Finally, a brief summary or an abstract covering the most important information in the report is usually attached.

The organizational format for all experimental research reports is basically the same, regardless of the field of study in which the author is working. Some of the research fields treated in this book are listed here.

Education	Management	Biology	Sociology
Economics	Chemistry	Psychology	Engineering
Agronomy	Animal Science	Language	Business

The purpose of this chapter is to show you the basic format writers in these fields use to report the findings of their studies and to give you practice in recognizing the components that make up the format.

INFORMATION CONVENTIONS

The following diagram illustrates the major sections of a typical experimental research report in the order in which they are usually presented. The diagram also shows the chapters in this book that deal with each of the sections.

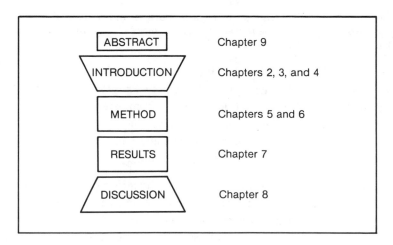

FIGURE 1.1 Typical sections of the experimental research report.

The Experimental Research Report—An Example

To help you understand the basic format of the experimental research report, we present here a report originally published in a professional journal. The report describes a study carried out in the field of agricultural education. The study evaluates the effectiveness of using microcomputers to teach economic principles to university students in a graduate course.

USING MICROCOMPUTERS IN TEACHING

Norman F. Rohrbach, District Supervisor
Missouri Department of Elementary and Secondary Education
Jefferson City, Missouri

Bob R. Stewart, Professor
Agricultural Education
University of Missouri-Columbia

Abstract—Although microcomputers are now common in classrooms throughout the United States, it is not clear what their most effective role is in the teaching-learning process. This study compared the effects of microcomputer-assisted instruction and traditional lecture-discussion on the performance of graduate students enrolled in an agricultural education course. Students in the control group performed significantly better on a written test than either of the two treatment groups. Students having previous experience with computers did not perform significantly better than those new to computer-assisted instruction. Further research needs to be conducted to determine the most appropriate place for computer-assisted instruction in agricultural education.

During the past 40 years, the United States has experienced the integration of the computer into society. Progress has been made to the point that small, inexpensive computers with expanded capabilities are available for innumerable uses. Many schools have purchased and are purchasing microcomputers for infusion into their directed learning programs.

Most individuals seem to agree that the microcomputer will continue to hold an important role in education. Gubser (1980) and Hinton (1980) suggested phenomenal increases in the numbers of computers both in the school and the home in the near future. There are always problems with a sudden onslaught of new technology. Like any new tool that has not been fully tried and tested, the role of the computer is in question. How should the computer be used in the classroom? Should the computer be the teacher or used as a tool in the classroom in the same way as an overhead projector? Can teachers do a better job of teaching certain types of materials with the microcomputer than with conventional teaching methods? Will the microcomputer have different effects on students with varying levels of experience? Schmidt (1982) identified three types of micro-computer use in classrooms: the object of a course, a support tool, and a means of providing instruction. Foster and Kleene (1982) cite four uses of microcomputers in vocational agriculture: drill and practice, tutorial, simulation and problem solving.

The findings of studies examining the use of various forms of computer-assisted instruction (CAI) have been mixed. Studies by Hickey (1968) and Honeycutt (1974) indicated superior results with CAI while studies by Ellis (1978), Caldwell (1980) and Belzer (1976) indicated little or no significant effect. Although much work has been done to date, more studies need to be conducted to ascertain the effects of microcomputer-assisted instruction in teaching various subjects in a variety of learning situations.

The purpose of this study was to ascertain the effect of using microcomputer-assisted instruction as compared to a lecture-discussion technique in teaching principles and methods of cost recovery and investment credit on agricultural assets to graduate students in agricultural education (Rohrbach, 1983). This topic was identified as being of importance to teachers in providing them the necessary background to teach lessons in farm records.

Method

The study was conducted as a three-group controlled pre-experiment following the static-group comparison design (Campbell & Stanley, 1963). It involved the use of three experimental groups, including a control Group A, a treatment group consisting of beginner-level microcomputer users Group B, and a treatment group consisting of intermediate-level microcomputer users Group C (see Table 1.1).

Table 1.1   Design of the Study

A Control n = 21 persons	B Treatment n = 25 persons	C Treatment n = 16 persons
Lecture-discussion technique 2 two-hour class sessions Evaluation by written tests	Microcomputer-assisted instruction (no experience) Maximum of 4 hours for instruction Evaluation by written test Record of actual time used	Microcomputer-assisted instruction (intermediate experience) Maximum of 4 hours of instruction Evaluation by written test Record of actual time used

Population

The population for the study consisted of graduate students in agricultural education at the University of Missouri-Columbia. Participants in the study were enrollees in courses offered through agricultural education at the University of Missouri-Columbia during the summer of 1983. This provided 21 students for control Group A, 25 students for beginning microcomputer Group B and 16 students for intermediate microcomputer Group C. The assumption was made that the participants represented a sample of graduate students in agricultural education. Therefore, the findings and implications of the study should be generalized to the extent that future groups of students are similar to the participants.

The 21 students designated as the control group were taught using a lecture-discussion technique. Forty-one students were divided into two treatment groups to receive microcomputer-assisted instruction. The class consisted of two sections with placement determined by previous microcomputing experience. Students with the ability to run and edit software programs were assigned to the intermediate-level group, and the remaining students were assigned to the beginners group.

Demographic data were collected from all subjects in relation to age, teaching experience, and knowledge and use of principles and methods relating to cost recovery and investment credit. Prior experience with the information was calculated on a nine-point scale.

Before receiving instruction, each group was introduced to the study by giving them the same orientation to the procedures to be used. It was explained that the learning sessions would be followed with a written evaluation on the material presented. They were told that the evaluation score would not count toward their grade in the course, but that it was important that they do as well as possible.

The classes comprising the control group were organized into two-hour class sessions. The instructor used two-hour sessions on two consecutive days for teaching using a lecture-discussion technique. The written evaluation was given during the first hour of the third day.

The treatment groups were given general instructions about operating the microcomputer learning program and were told they could spend a maximum of four hours in the laboratory working with the microcomputer-assisted instruction. The instructor who taught the control group was in the microcomputer laboratory to respond to questions and monitor student progress. Students were given two days to complete the task, were asked to keep a record of the amount of time used, and were given the written evaluation during a one-hour time period of the third day.

Development of Materials and Instrument

The materials used in teaching principles and methods in cost recovery and investment credit with the lecture-discussion method have been in place for three years and were the basis for writing a computer teaching program. The microcomputer learning modules, written in BASIC Language for the Apple IIe microcomputer, contained the principles, methods, examples, objectives, problems and so forth to be learned by students in the segment of the class devoted to cost recovery and investment credit. The modules were designed to present the concepts using the same problems and examples used in the lecture discussion procedure. All teaching materials and related microcomputer learning modules were checked for technical accuracy by a professor of agricultural economics responsible for preparing inservice materials related to tax law changes, a professor of agricultural education responsible for inservice education in farm management and a graduate research assistant in farm management.

The evaluation instrument used in the study was developed to measure the attainment of concepts in the learning package. The written evaluation was subjected to the Kuder-Richardson 20 test which yielded a reliability coefficient of .89. Validity of each question was established by a panel of experts with experience in teaching the concepts related to the material. There were 29 questions on the test which were worth one point each.

Null hypotheses were developed to test the research questions of the study. A one-way analysis of variance was used to test the first null hypothesis of no difference in performance among the groups (Ho_1). Differences were isolated using the Scheffé post hoc procedure. A Pearson correlation coefficient was used to ascertain the relationship between time spent on microcomputer-assisted instruction and student performance (Ho_2). Demographic data were examined to ascertain the homogeneity of the control group and experimental groups. An alpha level of .05 was used in testing the hypotheses. The data were analyzed with the Statistical Analysis System library computer package at the University of Missouri-Columbia (Ray, 1982).

Results

The age, teaching experience, prior experience with materials and time on task varied somewhat among groups as shown in Table 1.2. Time on task was held constant at 200 minutes for the control group, but ranged from 30 to 221 minutes for Group B and from 45 to 180 minutes for Group C.

Table 1.2 Characteristics of Participants

	N	Age (years) Mean	Age (years) Range	Teaching Experience (years) Mean	Teaching Experience (years) Range	Relative Prior Experience with Materials Mean	Relative Prior Experience with Materials Range	Time on Task in Minutes Mean	Time on Task in Minutes Range
Control									
Group A	21	29.8	22-53	5.9	0-25	4.29	0-9	200	200-200
Treatment									
Group B	25	33.0	22-44	8.4	0-17	4.08	0-9	112.2	30-221
Treatment									
Group C	16	35.6	24-50	11.4	1-24	4.81	0-9	90.4	45-180
Total	62	32.6	22-53	8.3	0-25	4.34	0-9	136.3	30-221

To help explain differences in student scores, correlational coefficients were calculated to ascertain if there were significant relationships between scores on the test and the subjects' age, prior experience with material, and years of teaching experience. As shown in Table 1.3, there was a significant positive relationship between prior experience or knowledge of the material and test scores (i.e., more prior experience influenced a higher test score). When prior experience scores (from Table 1.2) were compared on a group-by-group basis, Group A was not found to differ significantly at the .05 level from Groups B or C (+ values of .212 for A-B and 4.93 for A-C).

Table 1.3   Correlation Coefficients for Test Scores with Prior Experience with Material, Age and Years of Teaching Experience

	(n)	Prior Experience with Material (r)	Age (r)	Years of Teaching Experience (r)
Control Group A	21	.639	−.522	−.447
Treatment Group B	25	.670	.166	.239
Treatment Group C	16	.658	−.102	.040
All Students	62	.563	−.242	−.162

Note. Critical value at the .05 level of significance = .25.

Each experimental group was given the same written test after being subjected to the lecture-discussion or microcomputer-assisted instruction sessions as outlined in the design and procedures of the study. Mean scores and general results from each of the three groups are presented in Table 1.4, and the results of the analysis of variance test are reported in Table 1.5.

Table 1.4   Test Scores of Control and Experimental Groups

	N	Mean Score	Standard Deviation	Low Score	High Score	Variance
Control Group A	21	21.19	4.996	11	28	24.962
Treatment Group B	25	14.16	5.080	7	26	25.807
Treatment Group C	16	16.25	6.923	7	29	47.933
All students	62	17.08	6.294	7	29	

Table 1.5   Analysis of Variance for Differences among Control and Treatment Group Scores

Source	df	SS	F	PR < F
Model	2	578.990	9.29	0.0003
Error	59	1837.598		
Corrected Total	61	2416.597		

The F value of 9.29, reported in Table 1.5, indicated a significant difference in group mean scores. The Scheffé test was used to isolate more specifically where those differences occurred. There was a significant difference between the control group and each of the CAI groups. There was not a significant difference found between the two CAI groups. The test scores from the control group were higher than from either treatment group.

A Pearson correlation coefficient of − .016 indicated no significant relationship between time spent with the microcomputer-assisted instruction and test scores of students.

Discussion

Our first hypothesis, that there would be no significant difference among group mean scores, was rejected. However, our second hypothesis, that there would be no significant relationship between the amount of time utilized by the students with microcomputer-assisted instruction and students' test scores, was not rejected.

The following conclusions are subject to the conditions and limitations of this study: (a) the lecture-discussion approach was more effective than the microcomputer instruction in teaching the application of principles and concepts; (b) experience with the microcomputer had no effect on test scores, so it appears that the microcomputer-assisted learning modules were as easy for the beginners to use as for the intermediate-level users; and (c) the amount of time spent by students subjected to the microcomputer-assisted instruction did not significantly affect their scores when given freedom to select the amount of time spent.

The influence of prior experience with the subject matter was examined in two ways. As expected, there was a positive correlation between experience and student scores. However, there was not a significant difference for prior experience between Group A and treatment Groups B and C. Therefore, it does not appear that prior experience with subject matter was a confounding variable in this study.

The findings indicated that the lecture-discussion method of teaching was more effective than the microcomputer-assisted technique in teaching the principles and concepts presented under the conditions described. Given a choice, students in the microcomputer groups spent less time than did the students in the control group. Students in the control group were taught during regular hours while the treatment groups participated during laboratory time.

Since most studies indicated that students using CAI have generally performed as well or better than students under conventional instruction, the implication is that the difference in performance found in this study should be carefully evaluated. The findings might have been different if all students had spent a minimum of four hours using the computer program. Additional studies should compare groups using a mix of traditional instruction and CAI and should require groups to spend a specific amount of time on task. The challenge for agricultural educators is to better utilize the capabilities of microcomputer assisted instruction in the learning environment.

References

Belzer, T. J. (1976). *A comparative study of a traditional lecture method and a group paced, multimedia, non-lecture method used in teaching college biology* (ERIC Document Reproduction Service No. ED 133 026).

Caldwell, R. M. (1980). *A comparison of using computer-based education to teach literacy and numeracy skills to CETA and non-CETA participants enrolled in programs of adult basic education* (ERIC Document Reproduction Service No. ED 194 721).

Campbell, D. T., & Stanley, J. C. (1963). *Experimental and quasi-experimental designs for research.* Chicago: Rand McNally.

Ellis, J. A. (1978). *A comparative evaluation of computer-managed and instructor-managed instruction* (ERIC Document Reproduction Service No. ED 165 705).

Foster, R., & Kleene, M. (1982). Opportunities with computer assisted instruction. *The Agricultural Education Magazine, 54*(7), 12–14.

Gubser, L. (1980). *Schools of education—a time for revolution* (ERIC Document Reproduction Service No. ED 195 524).

Hickey, A. E. (1968). *Computer-assisted instruction: A survey of the literature.* Newburyport, MA: ENTELEK.

Hinton, J. R. (1980). *Individualized learning using microcomputer CAI* (ERIC Document Reproduction Service No. ED 196 409).

Honeycutt, J. K. (1974). *The effects of computer managed instruction on content learning of undergraduate students* (ERIC Document Reproduction Service No. ED 089 682).

Ray, A. S. (Ed.). (1982). *SAS user's guide: Statistics.* Cary, NC: SAS Institute.

Rohrbach, N.F. (1983). *Microcomputer use in teaching graduate students in agricultural education.* Unpublished doctoral dissertation, University of Missouri-Columbia.

Schmidt, J. R. (1982). *Computer utilization of resident instruction at the land grant university.* Unpublished manuscript, North Central Computer Institute, Madison.

WHAT HAVE YOU OBSERVED?

1. How many major sections does this experimental research report contain? Are all of these sections indicated by headings? Which major section does not have a heading?
2. What kind of information does each major section contain? Do any major sections have more than one kind of information? Which ones?
3. How does the format of this report compare with the general model in Figure 1.1?

Formulating a Research Question

Although it rarely appears in the final report itself, the *research question* is the basis on which the study is planned and carried out. After researchers have focused on a specific topic of investigation, they formulate a question that addresses a specific aspect of the topic in which they are interested. For example, if a researcher is interested in studying the effect of industrial pollution on plant life in a particular area, he or she might formulate a question like the following:

RESEARCH QUESTION: What are the effects of increased concentrations of sulfuric acid in the atmosphere
on production of grain sorghum?

Asked another way, the same topic could be addressed through a different
question:

RESEARCH QUESTION: Do increased concentrations of sulfuric
acid in the atmosphere lead to significant
decreases in the production of grain sorghum?

Formulating a Hypothesis

In formal research work, it is necessary to formulate a statement of expected
results. This is called the *hypothesis*. The hypothesis is a possible response to the
research question. For example, a hypothesis based on the research question in
the previous section might look like this:

HYPOTHESIS: Abnormally high concentrations of sulfuric acid in
the atmosphere have no effect on the production
of grain sorghum.

When the hypothesis is stated in this negative way, it is called the *null hypothesis*
(H_0). The purpose of the experiment is to determine whether the hypothesis can
be rejected or not. We take a closer look at how the research question (and the
hypothesis) is presented in the research report in Chapter 4.

EXERCISE 1.1   Analysis

Look back at the previous report on microcomputers in teaching. Determine
the *research question* and locate the *hypotheses*. Then write them out in the
following spaces.

1. Research Question: _____

_____

2. Hypotheses: _____

_____

_____

Are the hypotheses stated as *null hypotheses?*
Yes _____ No _____
(Remember that in many journal articles the hypotheses are not often stated ex-
plicitly, as they are in this article.)

EXERCISE 1.2 Analysis

A complete research report from the field of psychology is reproduced here as it appeared in a journal article. However, the *headings* and *spaces* that separated the original article into its major sections have been omitted. Read the report carefully and decide where each major section begins and ends. Then label each section with the appropriate heading.

BIAS IN EYEWITNESS ACCOUNTS:
THE EFFECTS OF QUESTION FORMAT, DELAY INTERVAL, AND
STIMULUS PRESENTATION

Thomas J. Lipscomb
Hunter A. McAllister
Norman J. Bregman
Department of Psychology
Southeastern Louisiana University

5

10

One of the three representations of a staged automobile collision was shown to 180 students from introductory psychology classes. We then questioned the students about details of the accident, using either marked or unmarked modifiers. Half the students were questioned immediately after viewing the stimulus material and half after a 20-min delay. The results indicated that estimates of the magnitude of a number of aspects of the collision were significantly greater when unmarked modifiers were used in phrasing the relevant questions. Students who were questioned after the 20-min delay gave significantly greater estimates of monetary damage than the students who answered immediately after viewing the representation. The nature of the stimulus material had inconsistent but significant effects.

15

20

25

In recent years, there has been a dramatic proliferation of research concerned with the accuracy and reliability of eyewitness reports. This research has documented the importance of a number of variables of which one of the most interesting and powerful is exposure to *postevent information*, which includes all additional related information to which a person is exposed after witnessing an event. Loftus and Palmer (1974) reported that the nature of questions asked a witness could systematically affect the report of details of that event. Subjects viewed films of automobile collisions and subsequently were quizzed about the speeds at which the vehicles involved were traveling. Speed estimates varied with the verb used in the interrogatory sentence. Specifically, estimates of the magnitude of speed were altered when the verbs *smashed, collided, bumped, hit,* and *contacted* were employed. These verbs were apparently interpreted as implying different degrees of contact and caused the different estimates. Similar results have been obtained by varying the adverb employed (Lipscomb, Bregman, & McAllister, in press). Loftus and Palmer have consistently argued that these effects are the result of an alteration of the memory of the witnessed event produced by the introduction of postevent information. Although such an explanation is consistent with available data, so too is a somewhat more parsimonious explanation.

The effect of postevent information embedded in the phrasing of the question may produce a response bias independent of memory alteration. This simpler explanation is tenable as the result of a study reported by Harris (1973). Harris obtained responses to questions that varied according to whether a "marked" or "unmarked" modifier was employed. An unmarked modifier implies that a property such as height or length possesses an indefinite upper limit. The marked modifier carries no such implication. Harris asked subjects to give numerical responses to a set of 32 questions employing 16 pairs of marked and unmarked adjectives and adverbs. For example, subjects were asked, "How heavy was the set of weights?" (unmarked) and "How light was the set of weights?" (marked). For 14 of the 16 modifier pairs, the subjects' mean numerical estimates were in the predicted direction. These were hypothetical questions, however; no concrete stimuli were involved, and therefore, there was no possibility that memory was involved.

Other research by Loftus, Miller, and Burns (1978) has revealed that a further variable affecting the reliability of eyewitness accounts is the time lapse between the event and the introduction of postevent information. Therefore, one might expect that modifiers used in a question introducing postevent information would have more influence on the eyewitness after a time lapse than modifiers introduced immediately after the event.

A final issue relevant to the present study is the nature of the stimulus material itself. Although voluminous studies of memory document the importance of this variable, little has been done to determine how the nature of stimulus material might affect eyewitness reports. It is reasonable to propose, however, that information presented in a more complete format would be less vulnerable to contaminating effects than material that was partial in nature.

The present study examined the role of three variables on estimates of details of an automobile collision. These variables were (a) the adjective used in phrasing a question (marked vs. unmarked), (b) the format of the stimulus material (a complete videotaped sequence or an incomplete videotaped sequence or an audio stimulus only), and (c) the delay interval (immediate or following a 20-min delay).

A 2 × 2 × 3 between-subjects factorial design was employed. A Sony video-cassette recorder/player (model SLO-340) and a 19-in, black and white video monitor were employed to present three representations of an automobile accident described previously by Bregman and McAllister (1982). The complete version lasted for 12s and depicted two automobiles colliding at an intersection. The sequence showed a station wagon (Car 1) striking a compact car (Car 2) in the right rear panel and the compact spinning around from the impact. The sequence was followed by a close-up view of the damage sustained by both cars in the collision. (At impact, both cars were traveling approximately 25 mph.) The sounds of engine acceleration and the impact of the collision were clearly audible. The abbreviated 8-s version showed the cars accelerating and colliding and contained the audio-only stimulus.

We recruited 180 students (90 males, 90 females) from introductory psychology classes. The students were divided into groups of three and were exposed to one of three types of stimulus material. They were questioned and debriefed individually. Half the students were questioned immediately after being exposed to the stimulus material, and the other half engaged in a filler activity (reading a *Reader's Digest* story) for 20 min prior to questioning. The students were asked to estimate the speed at which each of the cars was traveling at impact on a 5-point scale (from *very fast* to *very slow*) and to provide an estimate in miles per hour. The phrasing of the questions varied with the experimental condition; half were questioned using a marked adverb (*slow*) and half with an unmarked adverb (*fast*). Students then completed a parallel questionnnaire in a Likert-type format requiring responses on an 11-point scale. There were 13 questions, including some that related to physical damage, monetary damage, and personal injury. Each question employed either a marked or an unmarked adverb.

The data, analyzed by multivariate analysis of variance, resulted in significant effects for stimulus, $F(26, 314) = 1.93 \, p < .005$, and for modifier, $F(13, 156) = 3.124, p < .001$. Separate analyses of variance were then performed, yielding several significant effects. Estimations of the speed of both cars were significantly greater when the unmarked adverb *fast* was employed as compared to the marked adverb *slow* (see Table 1.6). Similarly, estimates of the extent of damage, skidding, noise, and harm to occupants were all significantly greater when the relevant questions were phrased with unmarked as opposed to marked adverbs (see Table 1.6). Students who were questioned after the 20-min delay estimated greater monetary damage to both cars than those who were questioned immediately following exposure to the stimulus material, $F(1, 168) = 5.5$, $p < .02$, for Car 1; $F(1, 168) = 8.93$, $p < .003$, for Car 2 (see Table 1.7). The speed of Car 1 was estimated to have been significantly greater by students who were questioned immediately following exposure. Exposure to the complete version of the stimulus exerted significant but inconsistent effects on estimates of damage to Car 2, $F(2, 168) = 3.36$, $p < .037$; noise, $F(2, 168) = 4.71$, $p < .01$; and skidding of Car 2, $F(2, 168) = 7.17$, $p < .001$.

Table 1.6   Mean Estimates and Analysis of Variance Summary as a Function of Adverb Employed

Question and unit of measurement	Modifier	M	F	p
How _____ was Car 1 going? (mph)	Fast[a] Slow	36.20 27.50	23.7	<.0001
How _____ was Car 1 going? (scale)	Fast Slow	3.62[b] 2.56[b]	3.93	<.05
How _____ was Car 2 going? (mph)	Fast Slow	39.76 35.25	5.86	<.017
How _____ was Car 2 going? (scale)	Fast Slow	3.52[b] 3.31[b]	4.08	<.05
How _____ damage was done to Car 1?	Much Little	6.27[c] 5.40[c]	9.43	<.002
How _____ were the skid marks made by Car 1?	Long Short	5.04[c] 3.88[c]	11.20	<.001
How _____ noise occurred as a result of the accident?	Much Little	7.44[c] 6.52[c]	7.62[c]	<.006
How _____ bruises do you think the driver of Car 1 suffered?	Many Few	5.22[c] 3.85[c]	13.16	<.0001
How _____ bruises do you think the driver of Car 2 suffered?	Many Few	5.27[c] 4.47[c]	5.35	<.022

[a]Unmarked adverb is reported first for each comparison. [b]Values could range from 1 to 5. [c]Values could range from 1 to 11.

Table 1.7   Mean Estimates of Speed and Monetary Damage as a Function of Delay Interval

Estimate	Immediate	Delay
Speed of Car 1	5.2[a]	4.6[a]
Monetary damage to Car 1	$659.27	$1,041.19
Monetary damage to Car 2	$688.96	$1,104.11

[a]Values could range from 1 to 11.

Results of the present study represent the most complete documentation to date that in obtaining estimates of aspects of a complex event from witnesses, the way a question is phased can dramatically affect the estimates. In the present study, the use of unmarked adverbs, implying no upper limit, resulted in higher estimates of the extent of property damage, personal injury, noise, and skidding. In fact, the unidirectional nature of this effect and the fact that it occurred across such a broad range of dependent measures is striking. The implication for the legal system is clear. Phrasing of questions by officers of the court may significantly affect various aspects of witnesses' verbal reports. The issue of whether this effect is the result of an alteration of the memory of the event, or due to a response bias operating independent of memory alteration remains unresolved. But our results suggest that this effect is the result of a response bias because no interaction between delay interval and the manner in which the question was phrased or between delay interval and stimulus format was obtained.

The results of the present study suggest two dimensions that might profitably be addressed by future researchers in the area. First, the delay employed in the present study was quite short (20 min). The use of longer delay intervals—days or weeks—might produce quite different results. Second, a more definitive test of whether effects of the manner in which a question is phrased are due to alteration in memory or are simply the result of response bias would be to include conditions in which no stimulus was present. If an effect is obtained with no stimulus, clearly that effect could not be due to memory alteration.

Bregman, N. J., & McAllister, H. A. (1982). Eyewitness testimony: The role of commitment in increasing reliability. *Social Psychology Quarterly, 45,* 181–184.

Harris, R. J. (1973). Answering questions containing marked and unmarked adjectives and adverbs. *Journal of Experimental Psychology, 97,* 399–401.

Lipscomb, T. J., Bregman, N. J. & McAllister, H. A. (in press). A developmental inquiry into the effects of postevent information on eyewitness accounts. *Journal of Genetic Psychology.*

Loftus, E. F., Miller, D. C., & Burns, H. J. (1978). Semantic integration of verbal information into a visual memory. *Journal of Experimental Psychology: Human Learning and Memory, 4,* 19–33.

Loftus, E. F. & Palmer, J. C. (1974). Reconstruction of automobile destruction: An example of the interaction between language and memory. *Journal of Verbal Learning and Verbal Behavior*, *13*, 585–589.

EXERCISE 1.3 Library

1. Find the name of a *professional journal* in your field of study that publishes reports of experimental research.
2. Go to your library and locate this journal in the list of *serial holdings*. Write down the library *call number* for the journal.
3. Find a recent issue of the journal and locate in it an article reporting on a topic that interests you and that you can understand. Photocopy the complete article and write down all the bibliographic information: name of journal, year, volume number, and page numbers.
4. Examine your article in terms of its *general format*. Is the format similar to or different from the diagram in Figure 1.1 on page 3? In what ways does it differ?
5. Read the research report carefully and answer the following questions:
   a. What *research question* were the authors trying to answer?
   b. Can you formulate a *hypothesis* that would answer this question?
   c. What type of study did they design: controlled experiment, correlational study, survey questionnaire, or some other kind?
6. In your opinion, is the report well organized and easy to read?

INTEGRATION

EXERCISE 1.4 Writing Up Your Own Research

The best way to benefit from this book is to conduct an actual experimental research project and then to write up the results. Perhaps you are currently involved in a research project. If you are not, the following exercise will help you get practical experience in carrying out and writing up experimental research.

1. By yourself, or with a group of classmates, choose an area of interest that you would like to research. Limit this area to a *specific topic* that will produce numerical data. Following are some examples of possible research topics.

a. A survey of the most common adjustment problem encountered by different groups of international students on an American university campus.
b. An analysis of the most important language skills needed by international students at an American university (as perceived by students and/or their professors).
c. An inventory of the kinds of language errors considered most serious by professors in the written English of their students.
d. A determination of the kinds of factors international students take into account when they select a university to attend in a foreign country.

2. Write a *research question* that focuses on one aspect of your topic.
3. Formulate a *hypothesis* that is a possible response to your research question.
4. With the help of your instructor, design a study that will permit you to answer your research question.
5. Determine the type of *materials* you will need in order to carry out your study.
6. If necessary, ask an experienced researcher to check the hypothesis and design of your study, and to determine what kind of statistical analysis should be done to interpret your data.

CHECKLIST FOR CHAPTER 1

RESEARCH REPORT FORMAT

_____ Abstract.

_____ Introduction.

_____ Method.

_____ Results.

_____ Discussion.

STEPS IN BEGINNING THE RESEARCH PROCESS

_____ Select an area of interest.

_____ Focus on one aspect of the area.

_____ Write a research question.

_____ Formulate a hypothesis.

_____ Design the study.

2

INTRODUCTION: Establishing a Context

OVERVIEW

In this and the next two chapters we focus on the first part of the experimental research report, the **introduction**. The introduction serves as an orientation for readers of the report, giving them the perspective they need to understand the detailed information coming in later sections.

The introduction can be divided into five parts, or stages. In Stage I, the writer establishes a context, or frame of reference, to help readers understand how the research fits into a wider field of study. We examine and practice Stage I, *the setting*, in this chapter.

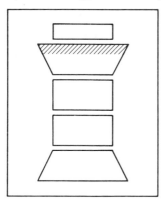

FIGURE 2.1   The setting (Stage I).

INFORMATION CONVENTIONS

The Five Stages

In order to better understand the function of Stage I, the setting, let us begin by briefly looking at all five stages of an introduction. Following is the introduction to the research report about computers in education that we saw in Chapter 1. Notice that it contains five distinct stages.

USING MICROCOMPUTERS IN TEACHING

Stage I

During the past 40 years, the United States has experienced the integration of the computer into society. Progress has been made to the point that small, inexpensive computers with expanded capabilities are available for innumerable uses. Many schools have purchased and are purchasing microcomputers for infusion into their directed learning programs.

Stage II

Most individuals seem to agree that the microcomputer will continue to hold an important role in education. Gubser (1980) and Hinton (1980) suggested phenomenal increases in the numbers of computers both in the school and the home in the near future. Schmidt (1982) identified three types of microcomputer use in classrooms: the object of a course, a support tool, and a means of providing instruction. Foster and Kleene (1982) cite four uses of microcomputers in vocational agriculture: drill and practice, tutorial, simulation and problem solving.

The findings of studies examining the use of various forms of computer-assisted instruction (CAI) have been mixed. Studies by Hickey (1968) and Honeycutt (1974) indicated superior results with CAI while studies by Ellis (1978), Caldwell (1980) and Belzer (1976) indicated little or no significant effect. Although much work has been done to date, more studies need to be conducted to as-

Stage III

certain the effects of microcomputer-assisted instruction in teaching various subjects in a variety of learning situations.

Stage IV

The purpose of this study was to ascertain the effect of using microcomputer-assisted instruction as compared to a lecture-discussion technique in teaching principles and methods of cost recovery and investment credit on agricultural assets to graduate students in agricultural education. This topic was identified as being of impor-

Stage V 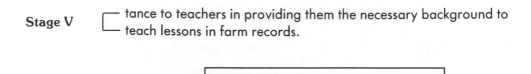 tance to teachers in providing them the necessary background to teach lessons in farm records.

WHAT HAVE YOU OBSERVED?

1. What do you think is the purpose of each of the five stages in this introduction?
2. Why do you think the writers put the five stages in this particular order?
3. Do you think this order of information could be used for writing introductions in other fields, or is it valid only for education?
4. Which stage is the longest? Can you see any reason for this?

Ordering your Information

The preceding example is typical of introductions to experimental research reports in many different fields in terms of (1) the *kinds* of information it provides to the reader and (2) the *order* in which the information is sequenced. Figure 2.2 illustrates this sequence.

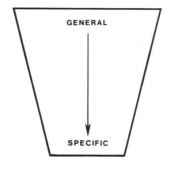

FIRST STAGE: General statement(s) about a field of research to provide the reader with *a setting* for the problem to be reported

SECOND STAGE: More specific statements about the aspects of the problem *already studied* by other researchers

THIRD STAGE: Statement(s) that indicate *the need for more investigation*

FOURTH STAGE: Very specific statement(s) giving *the purpose/objectives* of the writer's study

FIFTH STAGE: Optional statement(s) that give a *value* or *justification* for carrying out the study

FIGURE 2.2   The fives stages of the introduction.

EXERCISE 2.1   Analysis

Following is an example of an introduction from the field of psychology. After reading it, identify which sentences correspond to <u>four</u> of the five stages we have discussed.

EYE MOVEMENTS WHILE WATCHING A BASEBALL PITCH

[1]Many motor skills require action based on rapid change in the environment. [2]One such skill is baseball batting. [3]The baseball batter relies most heavily on vision for pertinent information. [4]Moreover, a good pitcher will attempt to give the hitter misleading cues during the wind-up and delivery. [5]Visual-search strategies must be used by a batter to sample relevant locations in the visual display so response can be made at the proper time.

[6]Research has shown that visual-search patterns can be governed by a variety of factors including experience. [7]Mourand and Rockwell (1972) examined the visual-search strategies used by six novice and four expert drivers. [8]Novice drivers sampled their mirrors and instruments more frequently than did expert drivers. [9]On the freeway, novice drivers made smooth pursuit movements while the experts made only eye fixations.

[10]Bard, Fleury, Carriere, and Halle (1980) examined the visual-search patterns of expert and novice gymnastic judges. [11]They found that the expert judges had 27% fewer fixations than novice judges. [12]Eye fixations also differed for novice and expert basketball players. [13]Bard and Fleury (1976) showed slides of typical offensive basketball situations to players and recorded their eye movements/fixations. [14]Expert players made fewer fixations than novices.

[15]The informational content of various portions of a baseball's trajectory from pitcher to batter has been debated but most of the research has focused on the terminal portion of the ball flight. [16]The purpose of the present study was to examine the visual-search strategies of expert and novice baseball players during the preparatory phase (wind-up and release of the pitch) of baseball hitting. [17]A second goal was to document the existence of an eye-movement reaction time prior to the eyes tracking the pitch.

Stage I (the setting):   Sentence(s) _____

Stage II (already studied):   Sentence(s) _____

Stage III (investigation needed):   Sentence(s) _____

Stage IV (purpose):   Sentence(s) _____

Stage V (value) does not appear in this report.

Writers do not always arrange the stages of their introductions in this exact order. Sometimes a writer interrupts one stage with another, and then returns to the earlier stage. Sometimes Stage II (usually called "The Review of Literature") is completely separate from the rest of the introduction. (In theses and dissertations, for example, it is often written as a separate chapter.) Stage V is often omitted entirely, as we saw in the preceding example. However, the general plan given here is very common and is the easiest for the beginning research writer to use.

Inventing the Setting

You should write the setting (Stage I) of your introduction so that it provides your readers with the background necessary to see the particular topic of your research in relation to a general area of study. In order to do this, start with obvious, generally accepted statements about the area in which you are working. Then, step by step, move the reader closer to your specific topic. You may do this in just a few sentences or in several paragraphs.

You can think of this stage as a process of first, establishing a "universe" for your readers; then, isolating one "galaxy" within this universe; and finally, leading your readers to one "star" in the galaxy. That "star" is your specific topic. In the example about baseball, the universe is "motor skills," the galaxy is "baseball batting," and the star is "visual-search strategies of batters."

STAGE I: The Setting

1. Begin with accepted statements of fact related to your *general area* (your "universe").
2. Within the general area, identify one *subarea* (your "galaxy" which includes your topic).
3. Indicate your *topic* (your "star").

EXERCISE 2.2 Analysis

Following is an example of Stage I from the introduction to a research report about waste-water treatment. Read the selection and then answer the questions which follow.

THE USES OF DUCKWEED IN WASTE-WATER TREATMENT

[1]Clean water is a basic human need. [2]Its discovery, transport, and systematic renewal have always been crucial to all but the least densely populated societies. [3]Increasing population and industrial wastes, together with diminishing sources of easily available energy with which to manage them, are converging to emphasize that all the earth's resources are finite. [4]But the supply of clean water, though also finite, is at least infinitely renewable.

[5]Among the various approaches to improving present technologies for waste-water treatment, several involve the use of plants, which can remove pollutants and provide materials useful as animal feeds or energy sources. [6]Various aquatic plants are being proposed in such approaches, and the duckweeds in particular, an essentially unique group of higher aquatic plants, might be especially advantageous in such systems.

---

1. Which sentences in the preceding introduction make obvious statements or statements that would be accepted as fact concerning the general area?

   _____

2. Which sentence focuses on one subarea of the general area of study?

   _____

3. Which sentence indicates the authors' topic?

   _____

Linking Ideas through Old and New Information Order

To lead readers smoothly through the ideas in Stage I, writers link sentences by making use of *old* and *new information*. This is done by placing old information—that is, information already known to the reader—at the beginning of sentences and placing new information at the end.

OLD/NEW INFORMATION ORDER

Plants obtain atmospheric CO_2 required for photosynthesis by diffusion through open leaf stomates.

Old	New
While this is taking place,	water in the leaf parenchyma tissues evaporates into the substomatal cavities and diffuses through the open stomates into the atmosphere.
This process	can create large water potential differences between the leaves and the soil surrounding the roots.

EXERCISE 2.3 Analysis

The following statements are adapted from the setting (Stage I) of an introduction to a research report about ice on rivers. The sentences are not presented in their correct order. Do the following:

1. Number the sentences in the order you believe they appeared in the original introduction, using old information and level of generality to guide you.
2. For each sentence, indicate whether it makes a statement about the general area, a subarea, or the author's topic.

RIVER ICE

A. _____ Water regularly changes back and forth from liquid to gas to solid.

B. _____ River ice constitutes a small fraction of the total quantity of ice in the world.

C. _____ The solid phase of water takes many forms.

D. _____ Water is one of the most important substances on earth.

E. _____ Solid forms of water range from small snowflakes to immense polar ice caps.

F. _____ Water makes man's survival possible and supports his transportation needs.

3. Now go back and underline the <u>old information</u> in sentences 2 through 6.

EXERCISE 2.4   Library

In the library, locate a journal article, thesis, or dissertation reporting research findings in ̣ ̣ ̣ ̣ ̣ ̣ ̣ ̣ ̣ ̣ ̣ ̣ oduction (the setting), photocopy ̣ ̣ ̣ ̣ ̣ ̣ ̣ ̣ ̣ questions:

1. Does the intro ̣ ̣ ̣ ̣ ̣ ̣ ̣ ̣ ̣ ̣ ̣ ̣ es does it consist of?

2. Does the Stag ̣ ̣ ̣ ̣ ̣ ̣ ̣ ̣ ̣ ̣ cussed here? Identify which ̣ ̣ ̣ ̣ ̣ ̣ ̣ ̣ kinds of statements sh ̣ ̣ ̣

3. Do any of the ̣ ̣ ̣ ̣ ̣ ̣ ̣ ̣ ̣ ̣ o another work?

4. Does the auth ̣ ̣ ̣ ̣ ̣ ̣ ̣ ̣ ̣ ences to link ideas? Find so ̣ ̣ ̣

1 D G
2 F G
3 A G
4 C S
5 E S
6 B A

General and Specific Noun Phrases

As we have seen, Stage I of the introduction usually begins with factual statements about the general area which includes your specific topic. When you write these kinds of general statements, it is conventional to use nouns that refer to objects or concepts at the highest possible level of generality. English offers several ways to construct these general nouns, which we examine in this section.

SEE WHAT YOU ALREADY KNOW   Pretest

A Stage I selection is given here from the field of geology. Fill in the blanks with an appropriate word. Some blanks do not require filling in.

THE TRANSPORT AND SORTING OF DIAMONDS BY FLUVIAL AND MARINE PROCESSES

[1]In the late 1940s, production of diamonds from alluvial sources represented about 40 percent of the world total. [2]Thirty years later, alluvial diamond _____ had more than doubled, and despite _____ development of major new kimberlite mines, it still represented more than 30 percent of the total natural diamond production.[3] _____ economic importance of alluvial _____ is thus considerable, and it is further emphasized by the fact that _____ alluvial diamonds are of consistently higher quality than diamonds recovered from source kimberlites, and also because certain countries (e.g., Sierra Leone, Central African Republic), are economically dependent on _____ production of _____.

Generic Noun Phrases

Statements in the setting of an introduction tend to be general in nature. Instead of referring to specific things, they often refer to *entire classes* of things. When you write sentences that contain nouns referring to an entire class of things, you should use *generic noun phrases* to carry this meaning. Generic noun phrases refer to all members of a particular class of living things, objects like "alluvial diamonds," or concepts like "diamond production" in the previous example.

In English there are different ways to write generic noun phrases. If the noun is *countable*, you can make it generic by adding the plural marker -s and omitting any article, or by using it in its singular form with the indefinite article *a* or *an*.

> ### GENERIC NOUN PHRASES: Countable Nouns
>
> EXAMPLE: *Alluvial diamonds* are of consistently higher quality than *diamonds* recovered from *source kimberlites*. (plural)
>
> EXAMPLE: *A new diamond mine* may take several years before coming into full production. (singular, meaning "any new diamond mine")

When the noun you want to use is *uncountable*, you can make it generic by omitting any article. (Of course, uncountable nouns never take a plural *-s*.)

> ### GENERIC NOUN PHRASES: Uncountable Nouns
>
> EXAMPLE: Thirty years later, *alluvial diamond production* had more than doubled. (meaning "all alluvial diamond production")

EXERCISE 2.5 Analysis

Look at the first two sentences of a report from the field of psychology. Indicate if each of the generic noun phrases underlined is *countable* (plural or singular) or *uncountable* by placing a C or U above the phrase. The first one is done for you.

    U
[1]Happiness is one of the six human emotions said to be universally present and understood. [2]A smile, one of the expressions of emotion that appears to be universally exhibited and understood, is thought to be sensitive to social context and to be shaped by social factors.

In addition, English has a fourth way of forming generic nouns you should learn to recognize and use. *A countable noun in its singular form* sometimes carries the generic meaning when used with the definite article *the*. This kind of generic noun phrase is often used when referring to living creatures or familiar machinery and equipment.

GENERIC NOUN PHRASES: Countable Nouns with *the*

EXAMPLE: *The hummingbird* can be found in all areas of North America. (meaning "hummingbirds in general")

EXAMPLE: The United States has experienced the integration of *the computer* into society. (meaning "computers in general")

Specific Noun Phrases

We have seen that the first part of Stage I, the setting of the introduction, usually contains a large proportion of generic noun phrases. Later in the setting, you will probably find it necessary to refer to specific items and concepts in order to move the reader from the general area toward your specific topic. This requires the use of *specific noun phrases*—that is, nouns that refer to particular, individual members of a class rather than to the class as a whole. In English, nouns with this meaning can be written in several ways.

1. *Referring to assumed or shared information.* Use the definite article *the* if you assume your readers share knowledge of the specific thing you are referring to.

SPECIFIC NOUN PHRASES: Referring to Shared Information

EXAMPLE: In recent years the growth of desert areas has been accelerating in *the world*.

---

2. *Pointing back to old information.* Use the definite article *the* when referring to a specific thing which you have already mentioned (the first mention usually uses the indefinite article *a/an*).

```
┌─────────────────────────────────────────────────────────────┐
│                                                             │
│   SPECIFIC NOUN PHRASES: Pointing Back to Old Information    │
│                                                             │
│   EXAMPLE:   New Mexico Solar Energy Institute is developing │
│              a computerized diagnostic assistant for solar domes- │
│              tic hot water systems. The computer-implemented │
│              assistant will be used at naval shore facilities │
│              throughout the world.                          │
│                                                             │
└─────────────────────────────────────────────────────────────┘
```

3. *Pointing forward to specifying information.* Use the definite article *the* when the specific meaning is made clear in *a following phrase or clause.*

```
┌─────────────────────────────────────────────────────────────┐
│                                                             │
│   SPECIFIC NOUN PHRASES: Pointing Forward to Specifying     │
│                           Information                        │
│                                                             │
│   EXAMPLE:   The gas which is produced in the western states is │
│              used primarily for home heating.               │
│                                                             │
└─────────────────────────────────────────────────────────────┘
```

EXERCISE 2.6   Analysis

Look at this Stage I from the introduction to the study about river ice. Some of the specific nouns are underlined. For each underlined noun, identify the preceding or the following information which makes the meaning of the noun specific. Do this by drawing an arrow from the specifying information to the noun. The first sentence is done for you.

RIVER ICE

[1]Water is one of the most intriguing substances on the earth. [2]Not only is man dependent upon it for life, but it also has the interesting property that its freezing point is within the range of the earth's surface temperature variation for significant parts of the year. [3]Thus its state regularly changes back and forth from liquid to gas to solid. [4]The solid phase takes on a myriad of forms, from

small, fragile snowflakes to <u>the immense masses</u> of the Greenland and Antarctic ice caps, which contain 95% of the world's fresh water. [5]Of particular interest is that part of <u>the world's ice</u> which occurs on rivers.

Guidelines for Marking Generic and Specific Noun Phrases

If you are having difficulty determining which, if any, article to use before a noun or noun phrase, ask yourself the following sequence of questions:

1. Is the noun meant in a *general* or a *specific* sense? If it is *specific*, use "the" before the noun. If it is general, ask yourself a follow-up question:
2. Is the noun *countable* or *uncountable*? If it is *countable*, use *a* or *an* (singular) or *-s* on the end (plural). If it is *uncountable*, use Ø (no article or -s ending).

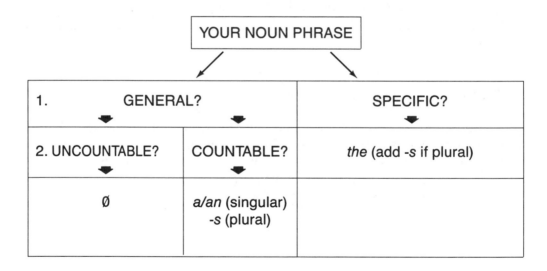

FIGURE 2.3

EXERCISE 2.7 Completion

Following is Stage I from a report in mechanical engineering. Fill in the blanks with the articles *a, an, the*, or the plural *-s* where necessary. Some of the blanks do not require filling in.

DESIGN OF ALUMINUM BICYCLE FRAMES

[1]Recent concerns about _____ expenditure of energy_ for human transportation_ have accentuated _____ need for more efficient passenger vehicle_ . [2]The result has been an unprecedented increase in _____ use of lightweight structural materials in _____ manufacture of automobile_ in _____ United States. [3]Another result has been _____ increased popularity of bicycle_ for practical transport.

[4]With _____ large interest in bicycle transportation, _____ research has been conducted at _____ University of California, Davis in recent years to develop ___ lightweight aluminum bicycle. [5] _____ Aluminum_ was chosen because preliminary calculation_ showed that weight could be reduced while increasing frame efficiency. [6] _____ Efficiency_ indicates _____ ability of a frame to absorb as small an amount of energy as possible from _____ total usable effort during pedaling. [7]Hence, ___ highly efficient frame delivers almost all usable rider effort to the drive train with very little energy going into _____ distortion of _____ frame.

Expressing Old Information

There are various ways you can state old information to connect back to the information in a previous sentence. One way is to simply repeat a word or to use a derived form of the word.

EXPRESSING OLD INFORMATION: Word Repetition and Derivation

EXAMPLE: Approximately three years ago, an apparently new and unexplained disorder called acquired immune deficiency syndrome (AIDS) was recognized. Characteristically, *AIDS* is associated with a progressive depletion of T cells.

EXAMPLE: Of interest is that part of the world's ice which occurs on rivers. Although *river ice* forms only a fraction of the total quantity of ice in the world, it has significance.

Another way you can indicate old information is to use pronouns and pointing words.

EXPRESSING OLD INFORMATION: Pronouns and Pointing Words

EXAMPLE: Water is one of the most intriguing substances on earth. *It* has the interesting property that its freezing point is within the range of the earth's surface temperature variation for significant parts of the year.

EXAMPLE: Ice forms when water is cooled to 0°C and continues to lose heat. Generally, *this* happens when the air temperature falls below 0°C.

Sometimes you can assume the reader knows the old information without your having to state it explicitly.

EXERCISE 2.8 Completion

Following is an excerpt from Stage I of a student thesis in civil engineering.
Fill in the blanks with the appropriate old information.

DEVELOPMENT OF A RAINFALL-RUNOFF MODEL

[1]Hydrology is based on the water cycle, most commonly
called the hydrologic cycle. [2] _____ is visu-
alized as beginning with the evaporation of water from the oceans
and continental lands. [3]The resulting _____
is condensed to form clouds, which in turn may result in precipitated water, or precipitation. [4] _____ which
falls upon the land is dispersed in several ways. [5]A large portion is
temporarily retained in the soil near where it falls and is ultimately
returned to the atmosphere by evaporation and transpiration of
plants. [6] _____ of the precipitated water,
called runoff, finds its way over and through the surface soil to
stream channels, while _____ penetrates
into the ground to become part of the earth's groundwater supply.

EXERCISE 2.9. Identification

Read the setting (Stage I) from an introduction to a report about the process of simulating rainfall in arid lands. Then go back and underline each noun phrase. Underline <u>generic noun phrases</u> once and <u><u>specific noun phrases</u></u> twice.

A PORTABLE RAINFALL SIMULATOR AND RUNOFF SAMPLER

[1]<u>Field research</u> on the interactions between soil and water commonly depends on natural rainfall or on some form of simulated rainfall. [2]Dependence on natural rainfall limits research because neither the timing nor the characteristics of a rain are known until it is over. [3]This problem is particularly serious in arid and semiarid areas where precipitation is infrequent and erratic. [4]With a rainfall simulator, an investigator can control the frequency, rates, and intensities of the rainfall in his studies.

EXERCISE 2.10   Fill-in

The Stage I paragraph about rainfall simulation is given below again. This time, without looking back at the original, fill in each blank space with the plural marker -s, a or an, or the where necessary. Some of the blanks do not require filling in.

A PORTABLE RAINFALL SIMULATOR AND RUNOFF SAMPLER

[1]Field research_ on the interactions between soil and

_____ water_ commonly depends either on _____ natural

rainfall_ or on some form of _____ simulated rainfall_ .

[2]Dependence on _____ natural rainfall_ limits research be-

cause neither _____ timing nor _____ characteristic_ of

a rain are known until it is over. **³**This problem is particularly seri-

ous in _____ arid and semiarid area_ where _____ pre-

cipitation_ is infrequent and erratic. **⁴**With _____ rainfall

simulator_ , _____ investigator_ can control the frequency,

rates, and intensities of _____ rainfall in his studies.

EXERCISE 2.11   Reconstruction

The same setting you have been practicing with is again given here, but
this time sentences are indicated only by lists of key words. Without referring to the original, try to reconstruct one sentence from each list. Add all
necessary words and word endings and write each group out as a complete sentence in the spaces provided. The key words are grouped and
listed in the correct order.

1. field research
   interactions between soil and water
   commonly depend
   natural rainfall
   some form of simulated rainfall

2. dependence on natural rainfall
   limit research
   because timing, characteristics of a rain
   not known
   it is over

3. particularly serious problem
   semiarid, arid areas
   precipitation
   infrequent, erratic

4. rainfall simulator device
   researcher
   control frequency, rates, intensities
   rainfall
   his studies

EXERCISE 2.12   Library

Refer back to the Stage I example that you found for Library Exercise 2.4.
In it, underline all <u>generic noun phrases</u> once and all <u>specific noun phrases</u>
twice. Circle(old information)and then answer the following questions.

1. What was the approximate ratio of generic noun phrases to specific noun phrases in your selection?
2. Which of the generic nouns you found were countable? Which ones were uncountable?
3. Of the countable generics, how many were written in the plural form? How many were written in the singular form with *a* or *an*? Did you find any countable generic nouns that were marked with *the*?
4. For each specific noun phrase in your example, find the reference either before or after the noun, or implied, that makes the noun specific.
5. Did the author use implicit old information?

INTEGRATION

EXERCISE 2.13   Guided Writing

So far in this chapter we have seen how to organize information in the introduction to an experimental research report. We have also seen how the first stage of the introduction, the setting, is written and what some of the language conventions are. In this exercise you will write your own Stage I. Your topic will be *World Food Shortages in the Next Decade*.

1. Imagine you are a researcher working for the Food and Agriculture Organization (FAO) of the United Nations. For the last year, you have been gathering statistical data that will allow you to predict the location and severity of food shortages for the coming decade. Your data include:

   per capita income
   gross national product   from selected countries of the world for the
   food production figures   past 20 years
   export and import figures

2. You must now write a report to be published by the U.N. stating your findings and making your predictions.
3. Suppose you have already organized and outlined the information for the other stages of the introduction to your report except Stage I. The other three stages will include the following information:

Stage II: Information already reported by other authors:
     FAO Reports from 1965, 1975, and 1985.
Stage III: Information still needed:
     World food supply predictions for the next 10 years.
Stage IV: Purpose of your study:
     To determine the location and severity of potential
      food shortages around the world in the coming decade.

4. In your setting (Stage I), you should establish a frame of reference for your readers, an orientation that will give them the perspective needed to understand your report. Some of the related ideas are listed here.

---

import/export balances   climatic changes
food: essential for human life   new technology
food shortages   population growth
social unrest   rich and poor countries
hunger

Select and sequence some of these ideas or add others of your own.

5. Now write your Stage I. Remember, the general tendency in an introduction is to move from general to specific ideas by progressing from a general area to a subarea to your topic. Also, remember to use old information as a linking device between sentences. Limit your setting to one or two paragraphs.

EXERCISE 2.14 Writing Up Your Own Research

Now that you have practiced writing the setting for the introduction to a research report on a topic of general interest, apply what you have learned in this chapter to the topic you selected for your own research project in Chapter 1. Write a setting (Stage I) for the introduction to your study.

Before you start writing, think about how you can best orient your readers to your specific topic. Remember, the setting should give them a frame of reference that will allow them to see how your topic fits into the wider "universe" of your general area. Restrict your setting to one or two paragraphs. To help you plan this section, consider the organization and language conventions we have studied in this chapter. Refer to the following checklist to help you remember these points.

CHECKLIST FOR CHAPTER 2

Introduction: Stage I

INFORMATION

_____ Move from general to specific statements.

_____ Begin with generally accepted statements of fact about an area of study.

_____ Identify one subarea within the general area which includes your topic.

_____ Arrange ideas in logical sequence.

_____ Use old information at the beginning of your sentences.

LANGUAGE

_____ Mark generic noun phrases appropriately:

      _____ plural -s;

      _____ a or an;

      _____ no article;

      _____ the.

_____ Mark specific noun phrases appropriately:

      _____ the.

_____ Indicate old information by using repeated or derived words, pronouns, or pointing words or by implying old information.

INTRODUCTION:
Reviewing
Previous
Research

OVERVIEW

In Stage I of your introduction you establish a setting for your research topic. In Stage II you review the findings of other researchers who have already published in your area of interest. For this reason, Stage II is often called the **review of literature**. It is essentially an organized collection of references, or *citations*, to other works which are listed in a separate section at the end of your report.

The review of literature serves three important functions. First, it continues the process started in Stage I of giving your readers background information needed to understand your study. Second, it assures your readers that you are familiar with the important research that has been carried out in your area. Third, it establishes your study as one link in a chain of research that is developing and enlarging knowledge in your field.

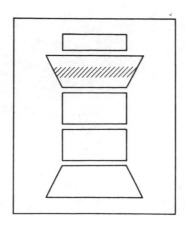

FIGURE 3.1   Literature review (Stage II).

INFORMATION CONVENTIONS

The following introduction is from a report in the field of ecology. Notice how Stage II supports the background information presented in Stage I.

SPATIAL DISTRIBUTION OF LITTER AND MICROARTHROPODS IN A CHIHUAHUAN DESERT ECOSYSTEM

Stage I

[1]In most deserts of the world, transitions between topographic elements are abrupt and watercourses which are dry most of the time tend to dissipate their occasional waters within local basins. [2]Occasional torrential rainfall, characteristic of most desert regions, washes loose debris into watercourses or transports this material, depositing it in and along the shores of ephemeral lakes. [3]These physical processes result in a redistribution of dead plant material (litter), affect the distribution of soil water and create a heterogeneous biotic community. [4]Therefore, before the dynamics of desert ecosystems can be adequately understood, the spatial relationships must be clarified.

Stage II

5There have been few studies of litter distribution and/or soil fauna in any of the world deserts (Wallwork, 1976). **6**Wood (1971) surveyed the soil fauna in a number of Australian arid and semi-arid ecosystems. **7**Wallwork (1972) made some studies of the microarthropod fauna in the California Mojave desert and Edney et al. (1974, 1975, 1976) studied abundance and distribution of soil microarthropods in the Mojave desert in Nevada.

Stage III

8In the Chihuahuan desert, Whitford et al. (1975, 1976, 1977) described the spatial relationships for many groups of organisms, but soil microarthropods remain unstudied. **9**The lack of such information represents a gap in our knowledge of desert ecosystems. **10**As part of our continuing program of studies of the structure and dynamics of Chihuahuan desert ecosystems, we designed the study reported here to understand the relationship between litter redistribution and the spatial distribution and composition of the soil microarthropod community.

Stage IV

WHAT HAVE YOU OBSERVED?

1. Notice that the writers of the preceding literature review cite other authors in two different ways. What are the two ways?
2. What do you think determines a writer's choice between these two forms?
3. What do you think determined *the order* of the citations in the preceding literature review?

Citation Focus

When you cite the work of other authors, you may choose to focus either on the *information* provided by that author, or on the *author him- or herself*. The first focus we call *information prominent* because the information is given primary importance. The author's name(s) and date of publication are parenthetically attached at the end of the sentence. More complete source information is found in an alphabetical list of references at the end of the paper.

```
┌─────────────────────────────────────────────────────────────┐
│                INFORMATION PROMINENT CITATION                 │
│                                                               │
│        ┌──────────────────┐        ┌──────────────────┐      │
│        │   Information     │   +    │    Reference     │      │
│        └──────────────────┘        └──────────────────┘      │
│                                                               │
│   In most deserts of the world, transitions                  │
│   between topographic elements are abrupt      (Smith, 1968). │
│                                                               │
│   The literature on teaching effectiveness has               │
│   established few theoretical grounds to guide               │
│   the selection of meaningful variables        (Doyle, 1978). │
│                                                               │
└─────────────────────────────────────────────────────────────┘
```

An alternate type of *information prominent* citation uses numbers between the parentheses (instead of author's name and date). The number refers to the alphabetical and numbered list of references at the end of the paper.

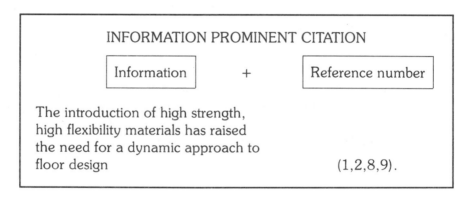

Information prominent citations are commonly used to signal the beginning of Stage II, where the citations refer to research in the *general area* of your study. (They may appear in Stage I as well.)

As the literature review continues, the citations refer to studies more closely related to your own. In this kind of citation, the author's name is given more emphasis. It serves as the subject of the sentence, followed by the date or citation number in parentheses, and then by the information. This kind of citation is called *author prominent*.

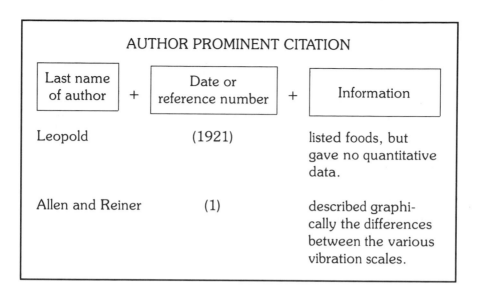

AUTHOR PROMINENT CITATION

Last name of author	+	Date or reference number	+	Information
Leopold		(1921)		listed foods, but gave no quantitative data.
Allen and Reiner		(1)		described graphically the differences between the various vibration scales.

EXERCISE 3.1 Analysis

Look back at the article about desert ecosystems at the beginning of this chapter. For each sentence (5 through 8) in Stage II, indicate whether the writers used *information prominent* or *author prominent* citations.

Sentence 5 _____

Sentence 6 _____

Sentence 7 _____

Sentence 8 _____

Order of Citations

It is possible to arrange your Stage II citations in order from those *most distantly related* to your study to *those most closely related*, as in the article on desert ecosystems. In addition, there are other ways to order your citations. For example, in a literature review describing the history of research in an area, you may arrange your citations in *chronological* order. Or, if you have a large number of citations to include in your literature review, as in a thesis or dissertation, you can group them according to the *different approaches* to the research problem taken by different authors. The citations within each group can then be ordered chronologically or from general to specific.

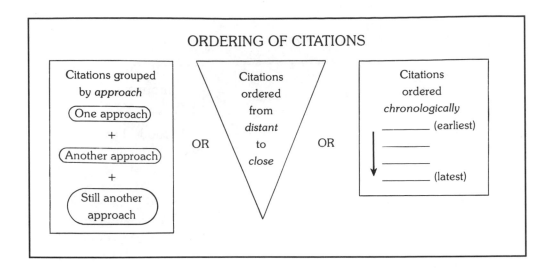

ORDERING OF CITATIONS

Citations grouped by *approach*

(One approach)

+

(Another approach)

+

(Still another approach)

OR

Citations ordered from *distant* to *close*

OR

Citations ordered *chronologically*

_____ (earliest)
_____
_____
_____ (latest)

EXERCISE 3.2 Analysis

Look at each of the following examples of Stage II. Indicate if the method of ordering citations used is *distant to close, chronological, different approaches*, or a combination of these methods. Read the title carefully to determine the *specific focus* of the author's own study.

A. PROVIDING DIRECTION AND BUILDING COMMITMENT: TEACHING AS INSTITUTIONAL LEADERSHIP

The conception of teaching as institutional leadership was first proposed by Waller (1932) who paid explicit attention to the organization of schools and the roles of teacher and student as defined by the organization. Recent literature on teacher leadership has not really followed Waller's approach of considering the roles of teachers and students in school organizations but has more closely resembled what Waller referred to as ''personal leadership''.

The literature on classroom leadership has also suffered from problems other than the tendency to deal with personal leadership. There has been a great deal of conceptual confusion about the dimensions of teacher behavior to be examined. Different investigations have used a variety of variables such as authoritarian-democratic (Lewin, Lippett & White, 1939), dominant-integrative

(Anderson, 1943), initiating structure-consideration (Hemphill, 1957), directiveness-warmth (Dunki & Biddle, 1974) task oriented-supportive (Cruikshank, 1976), and teacher structuring-praise (Soar & Soar, 1976).

Order of citations in example A:_____

B.   THE MEASUREMENT OF MOBILITY

The economic literature which discusses mobility and makes some attempt at measurement broadly falls into two categories. In the first, elementary statistical techniques and indices such as the rank correlation coefficient are used to evaluate the changes in relative positions (6, 8, 11, 13, 14, 19, 22). In the second category, measures of mobility are a by-product of simple stochastic specifications of changes over time (1, 9, 10).

Order of citations in example B: _____

C.   SUBSURFACE IRRIGATION AND FERTILIZATION OF
FIELD CORN

Little literature has been published on subsurface irrigation and fertilization through line emitters. Earl and Jury (4), Keng et al. (5) and others have examined water movement patterns and root development associated with trickle irrigation but in all cases emitters have been placed at or near the soil surface. Williams and Hanson (1) placed perforated plastic tubing 25 to 30 cm below cotton rows and over a 3-year period were able to achieve a 10% yield increase when compared to flood irrigation. Phene (9) described the use of line emitters for high frequency irrigation of sweet corn. Yield was 10% higher than obtained with sprinkler irrigation with the use of 50% less water. Mitchell et al. (7) irrigated field corn with perforated plastic tubing. Over a 3-year period yields with subsurface irrigation averaged 68% more than the non-irrigated control plots.

Order of citations in example C: _____

ON THE TIME CONSISTENCY OF OPTIMAL POLICY
IN A MONETARY ECONOMY

The time-consistency issue is by no means a new one in economics. Strotz (25) appears to be the first one to have raised it in relation to an individual consumer. More recently, however, Kydland and Prescott (15) have discovered a family of models exhibiting time inconsistency where the source of the problem lies in the technology and in the assumption that people hold rational expectations. Although they briefly touch upon a monetary economy, the central results of their remarkable paper are given in a context where money plays no central role.

In the monetary literature, Auernheimer (2) appears to be the first one to have noticed that time inconsistency could arise if the government attempts to maximize the revenue from money creation . . . (etc.)

Order of citations in example D: _____

```
┌─────────────────────────────────┐
└─────────────────────────────────┘
```

EXERCISE 3.3 Arrangement

The following citations are taken from Stage II of the introduction to a research report from the field of nutrition. The citations are given here in scrambled order. Number the citations in the order you feel they should appear in the literature review for this report.

```
┌─────────────────────────────────┐
└─────────────────────────────────┘
```

FOOD HABITS OF UNDERGRADUATE STUDENTS AT
NEW MEXICO STATE UNIVERSITY

A. _____ Young and Storvick (1970) surveyed the food habits of 595 college freshmen in Oregon and found that the men generally had better diets than the women.

B. _____ Litman et al. (1975) reported that green and yellow vegetables and liver (all nutritionally desirable foods) were not liked by teenagers in Minnesota public schools. They also found that teachers have almost no influence on their students' food habits.

C. _____ Studies of the food habits of young school children have shown that the diets of grade school children are often deficient in ascorbic acid, calcium and iron (Lantz et al., 1958; Patterson, 1966).

D. _____ A review of the literature indicates that food habit studies have been conducted with students from a variety of different age groups.

E. _____ Young (1965) examined the nutrition habits of a group of young school children and found that their mothers lacked information about the importance of milk and foods rich in ascorbic acid.

F. _____ Studies done with adolescent children report similar findings (Ohlson and Hart, 1970; van de Mark and Underwood, 1972).

G. _____ A number of studies have been conducted using both male and female college students as subjects.

EXERCISE 3.4 Library

In your library locate a journal article, thesis, or dissertation reporting research in your area of interest. Find Stage II (the review of literature), photocopy it, and answer the following questions:

1. Is Stage II written inside the introduction, as shown in our diagram (Figure 3.1), or is it placed in a separate section?
2. What is the ordering system of the citations (*distant to close, chronological, different approaches*, or a combination)?
3. Look at each citation and determine if it uses *author prominent* or *information prominent* focus. Does the author's choice of focus follow the conventions we have discussed in this chapter?
4. Which reference system is used in the Stage II citations: reference numbers, or author's name and publication date?

LANGUAGE CONVENTIONS

Citation Focus and Verb Tense

As we have seen, your decision whether to focus Stage II citations on the *information* or on the *author* determines the citation form you use. Similarly, this decision also helps to determine the *verb tense* you will use in each citation.

SEE WHAT YOU ALREADY KNOW   Pretest

In the following literature review from a report in the field of education, choose the best tense for each verb given in parentheses. Then write each verb in the tense you have chosen in the blank space provided.

NINTH GRADE ADJUSTMENT AND ACHIEVEMENT AS RELATED TO MOBILITY

Stage I

[1]Movement of families from one area to another is an accepted part of modern life (U.S. Census Population Reports, 1974).

Stage II

[2]The influence of this mobility on school achievement and adjustment (be) _____ the focus of several studies. [3]Yet findings concerning its effects upon school achievement so far (be) _____ inconsistent. [4]Bourke and Naylor (1971), in an early review of the literature, (find) _____ that 11 previous studies (report) _____ no effect of mobility on academic achievement, while 12 studies (find) _____ lower achievement. [5]More recent studies (note) _____ similar inconsistencies. [6]Goebel (1975) (ascertain) _____ that the rate of mobility (be) _____ not a significant factor in determining either short- or long-term academic performance. [7]Benson, Haycraft, Steyaert, and Weigel (1979) studying sixth graders (determine) _____ mobility to be

negatively related to achievement. [8]Likewise, Abramson (1974) and Schaller (1976) both (report) _____ that mobile students had lower academic performance.

     [9]Researchers (also study) _____ the relationship between mobility and classroom adjustment . . . .

Tense in Information Prominent Citations

When the focus of your citation is on the information, you should write the citation in the *present tense*. The present tense is used when the information you are citing is generally accepted as *scientific fact*.

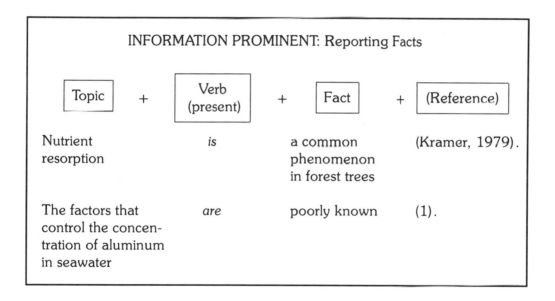

INFORMATION PROMINENT: Reporting Facts

Topic	+	Verb (present)	+	Fact	+	(Reference)
Nutrient resorption		*is*		a common phenomenon in forest trees		(Kramer, 1979).
The factors that control the concentration of aluminum in seawater		*are*		poorly known		(1).

NOTE: Some publications use only this citation form to credit sources.

Tense in Weak Author Prominent Citations

The *present perfect tense* is used in citations where the focus is on the research area of several authors. This kind of citation is called *weak author prominent*.

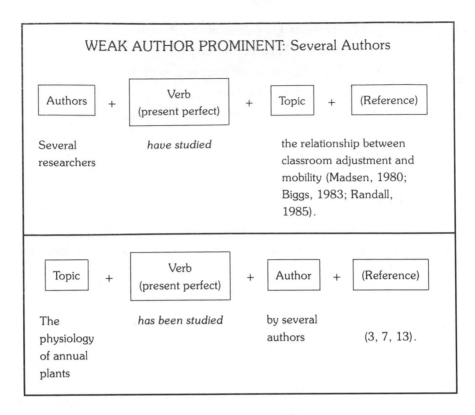

General Statements about the Research

The present perfect tense is also used in general statements that describe the *level of research activity* in an area. These statements are often written without citations.

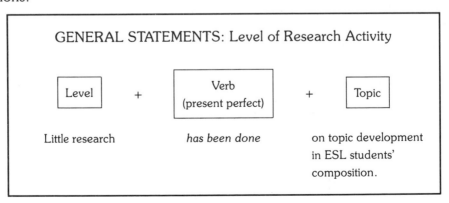

Information prominent citations, weak author prominent citations, and general statements are usually written at the *beginning* of Stage II, or at transition points at the beginning of *new sections* within Stage II.

Tense in Author Prominent Citations

Later in Stage II, you use author prominent citations to report the *findings of individual studies* closely related to your own. In these citations the *simple past tense* is used in the verb of report.

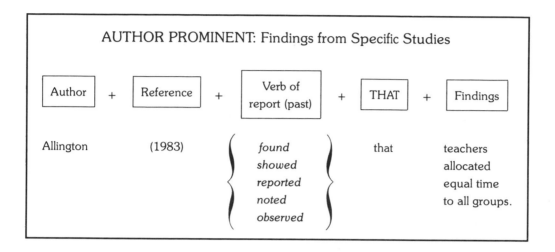

As you can see from these rules, the progression of verb tenses in your literature review follows the progression shown in the diagram below.

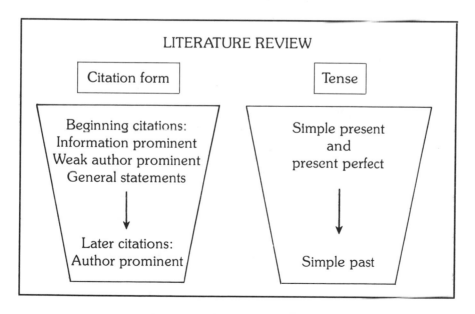

FIGURE 3.2 **Progression of tenses in Stage II.**

EXERCISE 3.5   Fill-in

In the following example from the field of psychology, fill in the correct tense for each Stage II verb given in parentheses.

LISTENING COMPREHENSION: THE EFFECTS OF SEX, AGE PASSAGE STRUCTURE AND SPEECH RATE

[1]The learning of verbal information is a two-stage process. [2]First of all the student must understand the meaning of the sentence he has just heard and then, secondly, he must relate the information it contains to what he has learned earlier and which is now stored in memory. [3]A number of authors (advance) _____ this active view of learning (Bartlett, 1932; Ausubel, 1968; Haviland and Clark, 1974; and Clark, 1976). [4]Other writers (show) _____ that this two-stage process operates at the level of sentences. [5]Barclay and Franks (1972) (show) _____ that when two or more sentences contain information about the same subject, the learner abstracts the information from the sentences and tends to integrate it into a whole.

[6]Riding (1975) (find) _____ that after listening to a prose passage in which some related details were in adjacent sentences, while others were separated by other sentences, ten-year-old children recalled the closely positioned details better than the more distantly positioned ones. [7]Kieras (1978) (study) _____ reading time in adult subjects using short paragraphs as the learning material. [8]He (note) _____ that reading time was less when a sentence was preceded by those containing related information than when one or more unrelated sentences intervened between directly related ones.

Attitude and Tense in Reported Findings

We have seen that the *focus* you choose helps to determine the tenses of the verbs in your literature review. Similarly, in author prominent citations your *attitude* towards the findings of the researchers also affects the complement verb forms in your Stage II sentences. You may feel that:

1. the findings of a particular study are generally accepted as *fact*;
2. the findings of a particular study are *limited to that study*, but are not to be accepted as true in all cases;
3. the author(s) of the study you are citing may themselves feel *tentative* about their findings; or they may not be reporting findings at all but only making *suggestions* or *proposals*.

Depending on which attitude you take towards the findings of the researchers you cite, you may use the *present tense*, the *past tense*, or various *modal auxiliaries*.

1. When you believe the findings you are citing are *fact*, use the *present tense* in the complement verb (that is, the verb in the part of the sentence giving the findings).

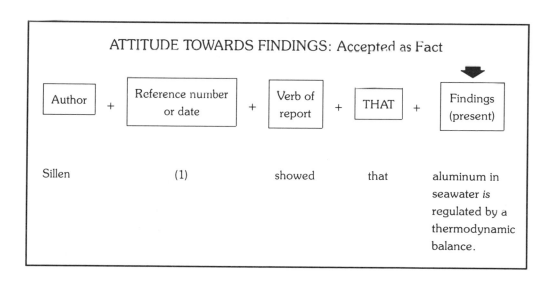

2. When you believe the findings are restricted to the *specific study you are citing*, use the *past tense* in the complement verb.

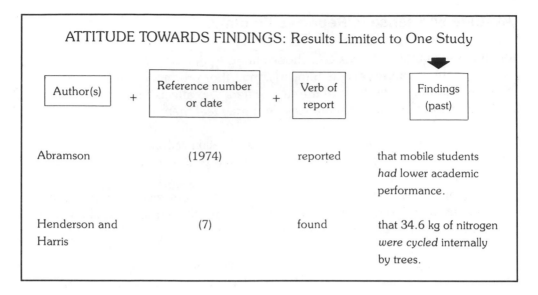

3. Finally, if the findings you are citing were seen by the original authors as *tentative*, or were only suggestions or proposals rather than findings, use *tentative verbs* for the verb of report, and a *modal auxiliary* with the complement verb.

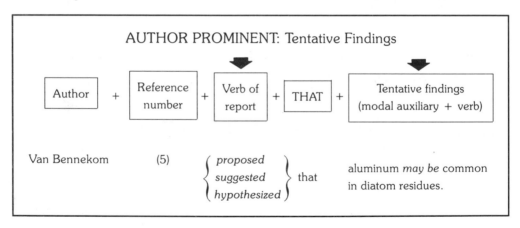

Notice that in all three of these cases, the verb of report is always in the *past tense*, while the verb tense in the "findings" part of the sentence varies according to the author's attitude.

EXERCISE 3.6 Transformation

Each of the following excerpts is taken from Stage II of a different experimental research report. In each case, determine if the author views the reported findings as *fact* or only *tentative*. Then rewrite each excerpt so that it indicates the opposite attitude.

---

a. _____ Several studies have shown that oats produce more forage than other winter cereal grains (4, 7, 13).

b. _____ The regulation of body temperature places demands on the respiratory system which exceeds the needs for gas exchange (Huffaker 1980).

c. _____ The magnetic field may affect both the velocity and temperature distributions of a conducting fluid between two parallel disks (Battaiah et al., 1979).

d. _____ A recent survey suggested that the public may be willing to consider the use of solar systems largely because of their low operating costs (3).

e. _____ Heimeann (1961) reported that sodium applications cause an increase in potassium uptake.

EXERCISE 3.7   Identification

Read the following literature review from the field of finance. Identify all verbs—both verbs of report and complement verbs. Underline <u>present tense verbs</u> once, <u>past tense verbs</u> twice, and <u>present perfect verbs</u> three times. Circle any (tentative verbs) or (modal auxiliaries) that you find.

NONSTATIONARITY AND EVALUATION OF MUTUAL FUND PERFORMANCE

[1]Several authors have evaluated the performance of mutual funds. [2]Keynor (17) and Sharpe (15) developed performance measures for establishing relative rankings for such funds. [3]Treynor

and Mauzi (18) devised a statistical test for determining whether mutual funds can anticipate major fluctuations in the stock market. [4]Jensen (7) proposed that an absolute measure of mutual fund performance could be used to determine whether mutual funds earn higher or lower returns than those expected for the level of risk associated with their portfolios. [5]Although these studies have examined mutual fund performance, none has employed an analytical framework for dealing with the fluctuations which may exist in the risk-return relationship for such funds (13).

<hr>

EXERCISE 3.8 Fill-in

The literature review about mutual funds is given here again. This time, without looking back at the original, fill in each blank with an appropriate verb or modal auxiliary. Select your verbs and verb tenses according to the rules you have studied in this chapter.

<hr>

NONSTATIONARITY AND EVALUATION OF MUTUAL FUND PERFORMANCE

[1]Several authors _____ the performance of mutual funds. [2]Keynor (17) and Sharpe (15) _____ performance measures for establishing relative rankings for such funds. [3]Treynor and Mazuy (18) _____ a statistical test for determining whether mutual funds _____ anticipate major fluctuations in the stock market. [4]Jensen (7) proposed that an absolute measure of mutual fund performance _____ be used to determine whether mutual funds earn higher or lower returns than those expected for the level of risk associated with their portfolios. [5]Although all of these studies _____ mutual fund performance, none _____ an analytical framework for dealing

with the fluctuations which may exist in the risk-return relationships for such funds. (13).

EXERCISE 3.9 Reconstruction

The same literature review you have been practicing with is again given here, but this time the sentences are indicated only by lists of key words. Without referring to the original, reconstruct one sentence from each list. Add all necessary words and word endings, and write out each group as a complete sentence. The key words are grouped and listed in the correct order.

---

1. several authors
   evaluate
   performance of mutual
      funds

2. Keynor (17), Sharpe (15)
   develop
   performance measures
   establishing relative
      rankings for such funds

3. Treynor and Mauzi (18)
   devise
   statistical test
   determine whether
   mutual funds
   anticipate
   major fluctuations
   stock market

4. Jensen (7)
   propose
   absolute measure of mutual
      fund performance
   be used
   determine whether
   mutual funds earn higher or
      lower returns than those
      expected

5. although all of these studies
   examine
   mutual fund performance,
   none
   employ
   analytical framework

EXERCISE 3.10 Library

Reread the literature review example that you used for the previous library exercise. In it, underline the <u>verbs of report</u> and the <u>complement verbs</u> in each sentence. Identify the tense of each verb you find and explain why the author(s) chose it. Determine if your author(s) followed the language conventions we have studied for Stage II.

EXERCISE 3.11 Analyzing Bibliography Conventions

There are several different conventions for constructing a bibliography (list of references). To learn the one you should use, go to the library and find a journal in your field. Photocopy the reference page from an article and analyze the *order* of information elements and the *punctuation* (including capitalization) that is used. Analyze one bibliographic entry for each of the following types of references:

1. a journal article;
2. a book;
3. an edited volume.

You may want to check with a professor in your department or with the graduate school at your university to see if a particular bibliography style is required.

INTEGRATION

EXERCISE 3.12 Guided Writing

Here you are given a background paragraph (Stage I) from the introduction to a research report about students learning English as a second language. The final part of the introduction (Stages III, IV, and V) is also given. Stage II, the literature review, is represented in *outline form*. Using the information in the outline, write a literature review appropriate for this introduction. Refer to the list of references at the end of the outline for your citation information.

DIFFERENTIAL GAIN RATES IN INTENSIVE ESL PROGRAMS: WHO GAINS THE MOST?

Stage I

Students entering intensive English as a second language programs at various proficiency levels may make comparatively greater or lesser gains in proficiency over the same period of training. The problem of predicting rates of progress is particularly interesting for teachers and administrators in intensive programs where some of the students have had little or no previous instruction in English language skills, but where all students are preparing to take university courses in English after a brief period of language instruction. The organization and teaching strategies of such a program are crucial to the future academic success of the students.

Stage II

Literature Review

A. Several studies—individual characteristics of language learners, environmental variables (classroom, school, community)

   1. CARROLL: Affective variables of students—predict success in foreign language learning?
     Findings: a. motivation—yes
             b. aptitude—yes
             c. IQ—no

   2. FATHMAN: External variables—affect the successful learning of English as a second language?
     Findings: a. class size—yes
             b. school size—yes
             c. school location (urban/rural)—yes

B. Other studies—use standardized English language tests to predict students' academic success

   1. MASON: Compare students' initial scores on Michigan Test of English Language Proficiency with students' grade point average (GPA) after one year
     Findings: Michigan not a good predictor

2. MORAN and ERION: Use *Comprehensive English Language Test* (CELT) as a possible predictor of students' academic success in university classes
Findings: CELT predicts GPA— no
CELT predicts number of credits earned—yes

C. Effect of students' initial proficiency on later progress in English—few studies

1. NEVO, SIM and BENSOUSAN: Non-intensive English program, Middle Eastern university
Findings: Students with higher initial scores on proficiency test—more progress than students with lower scores

2. MARTON: Non-intensive English program in Scandinavian university
Findings: results similar to Nevo et al.

Stage III

However, little information is available in the literature on predicting success of students enrolled in intensive English programs in this country.

Stage IV

This study was carried out in order to determine if students' scores on two standardized tests of English language proficiency could serve to predict whether they would make greater or lesser progress in English during a one-year intensive program. It was hoped that a systematic analysis of relative rates of progress among beginning, intermediate and advanced students would

Stage V

indicate if the program was benefiting some types of students more than others. Significant differences in progress, if found, would indicate the need for a thorough re-examination of program organization and instruction.

REFERENCES

Carroll, John B. 1962. The prediction of success in intensive foreign language training. In *Training Research and Education*, R. Glaser (Ed.). Pittsburgh: University of Pittsburgh Press.

Fathman, A. K. 1976. Variables affecting the successful learning of English as a second language. *TESOL Quarterly* 10:433–441.

Marton, F. 1972. The tenth year of English: review of a project concerning second language learning at university level. *Higher Education* 1:93–109.

Mason, C. 1971. The relevance of intensive training in English as a second language. *Language Learning* 21:197–204.

Moran, R. and J. G. Erion. 1978. Predictive validity of the CELT. *TESL Reporter* 11(3):1–3.

Nevo, B., D. Sim and M. Bensousan. 1977. The rich get richer and the poor get poorer. *System* 5:33–37.

EXERCISE 3.13   Writing Up Your Own Research

Now that you have written the Stage II (literature review) for the introduction to a research report about students in an English language program, apply what you have learned in this chapter to your own research topic. Write a Stage II for the individual or group research project you chose to conduct in Chapter 1. Follow these steps:

1. Visit your library and find at least *six sources* that relate to your proposed study. Your teacher or the reference librarian can help you locate appropriate sources.

2. Write down on note cards relevant information from the sources you have found. Include the *research topic* and the *findings* from each study and any other information you consider important. Also note all *bibliographic information* you will need to include in your list of references.

3. Decide how you will *order* the citations in your Stage II (for example, distant-to-close, chronologically, different approaches (or a combination of these), and organize your note cards in this order.

4. Using these notes, write your Stage II. Do not copy directly from your sources; paraphrase the authors' ideas. Refer to the following checklist to help you remember the conventions for Stage II we have studied in this chapter.

When you have finished writing your Stage II, put it together with the Stage I you wrote in the previous chapter. You may want to make some changes in the setting based on the information you have added in the literature review. Show these first two stages of your introduction to your instructor or research team members to get their reactions.

CHECKLIST FOR CHAPTER 3

Introduction: Stage II

INFORMATION

_____ Use a logical plan to order your citations.

_____ Use information prominent and weak author prominent citations at the beginning and at transitional points in Stage II.

_____ Use author prominent citations to report specific findings later in Stage II.

LANGUAGE

_____ Use verb tenses correctly:

    _____ present tense for facts;

    _____ present perfect tense for weak author citations and general statements about the research;

    _____ past tense for author prominent citations and results limited to a single study.

_____ Use tentative verbs of report for suggestions or proposals.

_____ Use modal auxiliaries in the complement to indicate tentative findings.

INTRODUCTION:
Advancing to
Present Research

OVERVIEW

After you have presented a contextual setting and discussed the previous work of other researchers, you use the final part of the introduction to focus the attention of the reader on the **specific research problem** you will be dealing with in the body of your report. This is done in three additional stages, which we designate as III, IV, and V. Stage III indicates an area that is *not treated* in the previous literature, but that is important from the point of view of your own work; Stage IV formally announces *the purpose* of your research; and Stage V indicates possible *benefits or applications* of your work.

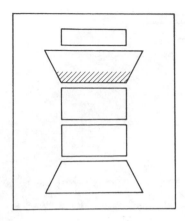

FIGURE 4.1   Advancing to present research (Stages III, IV, and V).

INFORMATION CONVENTIONS

Look at the following model introduction, taken from a report in the field of home economics. Notice that Stages III, IV, and V have been indicated by brackets.

FOOD-BUYING PRACTICES OF UNIVERSITY STUDENT WIVES

[1]Food expense is one of the largest recurring items in the budgets of most families. [2]Today, food purchases take more than one-sixth (17.8%) of the total consumer disposable income in the United States (3). [3]This expenditure includes money spent for meals away from home as well as for food bought for use at home. [4]Many demographic factors affect food-buying decisions, including age, education, income, and experience (10).

Stage III   [5]However, student wives are a specialized population group about which little is known.

Stage IV   [6]The purpose of this study was to learn more about the food-buying practices of wives of university students.

Stage V   [7]It is hoped that information from this study may be useful in identifying areas of weakness or lack of knowledge to those who are responsible for planning courses and programs in consumer education.

WHAT HAVE YOU OBSERVED?

1. What is the function of sentence 5?
2. How does sentence 5 relate to the previous sentences in this introduction?
3. What connection exists between sentence 5 and sentence 6?
4. What is the author trying to suggest about the research in sentence 7?

Ordering your Information

The kinds of information contained in Stages III, IV, and V are sequenced in order to move the reader logically from the literature review to the purpose of your study. We examine each stage individually to see how the information is presented.

Writing STAGE III: Missing Information

Stage III serves to signal the reader that the literature review is finished. It sums up the review by pointing out *a gap*—that is, an important research area not investigated by other authors. Usually Stage III is accomplished in only one or two sentences. Here are three alternatives you can choose from in writing your Stage III statement.

ALTERNATIVES FOR STAGE III

1. You may indicate that the previous literature described in Stage II is *inadequate* because an important aspect of the research area has been ignored by other authors.

2. You may indicate that there is an *unresolved conflict* among the authors of previous studies concerning the research topic. This may be a theoretical or methodological disagreement.

3. You may indicate that an examination of the previous literature suggests an *extension* of the topic, or raises *a new research question* not previously considered by other workers in your field.

In indicating some kind of gap left by earlier studies, Stage III prepares the reader for your own study.

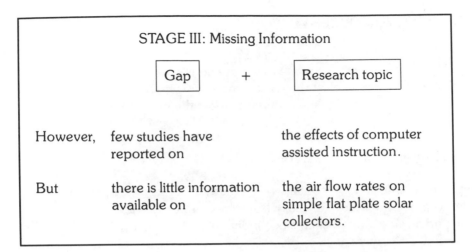

STAGE III: Missing Information

Gap + Research topic

| However, | few studies have reported on | the effects of computer assisted instruction. |
| But | there is little information available on | the air flow rates on simple flat plate solar collectors. |

EXERCISE 4.1 Analysis

An entire introduction from a research report in the field of business and finance is reproduced here. First read the introduction, then answer the questions that follow.

CONCEPTS OF BUSINESS AND FINANCIAL RISK

[1]There is considerable current interest in methods of limiting the business risk to which farmers are exposed. [2]Some approaches to business risk modification involve insurance, government programs, weather modification, and innovations of individual farmers.

[3]It is recognized that the introduction or modification of risk in the production process affects the pattern of resource allocation and in turn the level of production (Dillon 1979, pp. 102–48; Just, Wiens, and Wolgen 1980). [4]We suggest that there is also a financial response to business risk modification. [5]The difference is important in that business risk and financial risk may well be trade-offs in the risk behavior of farmers. [6]Thus, a decline in business risk

would lead to the acceptance of greater financial risk, reducing the effects of the diminished business risk on total risk.

[7]While most of the literature on risk and risk response treats only production and price risk (i.e., business risk), we intend to introduce the notion of financial risk explicitly into the decision-making process. [8]In this paper we present a conceptual framework for linking production and investment decisions to the financing decision via a risk constraint.

---

1. Which sentence in the preceding introduction contains Stage III?

   Sentence _____

2. Does the entire sentence correspond to Stage III, or only part of the sentence?

   All _____   Part _____

3. What word helped you recognize the beginning of Stage III?

   _____

Writing Stage IV: The Statement of Purpose

Stage IV serves to state as concisely as possible the specific objective(s) of your research report. This stage, *the statement of purpose*, thus follows directly from Stage III because it answers the need expressed in Stage III for additional research in your area of study.

You may write the statement of purpose (Stage IV) from one of two alternative orientations:

1. The orientation of the statement of purpose may be towards the *report* itself—that is, it may refer to the paper (thesis, dissertation, or report) that communicates the information about the research.

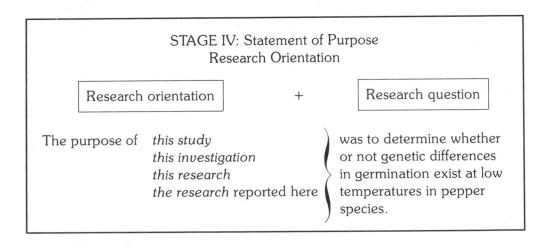

STAGE IV: Statement of Purpose
Report Orientation

Report orientation	+	Research question

The purpose of *this thesis*
The aim of *the present paper*
The objective of *this report*

is to determine whether an automatic measurement system can be applied to educational settings.

2. Or the orientation of the statement of purpose may be towards the *research activity*, in other words the study itself, rather than the written report.

STAGE IV: Statement of Purpose
Research Orientation

Research orientation	+	Research question

The purpose of   *this study*
this investigation
this research
the research reported here

was to determine whether or not genetic differences in germination exist at low temperatures in pepper species.

EXERCISE 4.2   Analysis

Do the following tasks.

1. Look at the introduction about business and financial risk in Exercise 4.1 and identify the sentence that contains Stage IV, the statement of purpose. Is its orientation towards the report or the research?

    Sentence _____ Orientation _____

2. Now look at each of the Stage IV examples that follow. Each is taken from a different research report. Determine whether each excerpt is an example of *research* or *report* orientation. Then write the word "research" or "report" in each blank space, depending on the orientation of the excerpt.

_____

a. _____ This paper describes the results of aerial surveys and interviews conducted in Honduras to determine the distribution and status of manatees in that country.

b. _____ In this paper we present a conceptual framework for linking production and investment decisions to the financing decision via a risk constraint.

c. _____ The present study was made to determine whether or not genetic differences in germination at low temperature exist in pepper species, and to establish the magnitude of such differences.

d. _____ The research reported in this paper was an attempt to develop an alternative analytical approach to machinery selection problems.

e. _____ The purpose of this article is to give the most direct answer possible to the direct question of how long advertising affects sales.

_____

Writing Stage V: The Statement of Value

In Stage V you justify your research on the basis of some possible value or benefit the work may have to other researchers in the field or to people working in practical situations. We can call this stage the *statement of value*.

Stage V is not included in every introduction. You should include Stage V in your introduction when you write a thesis, dissertation, or a thesis proposal. The statement of value is also commonly included in research reports written to describe a project conducted with money from outside sources. In reports written up as journal articles, Stage V is often omitted.

You may write Stage V from either of two alternative points of view.

1. The statement of value may be written from the point of view of the *practical* benefits which may result from applying the findings of your research.

STAGE V: Statement of Value
Practical Orientation

EXAMPLE A: This research may provide an alternative to the problem of manually demonstrating instrumentation principles in classroom environments.

EXAMPLE B: The results of this study could be useful to educators responsible for planning course work in consumer education.

---

2. Or you may write the statement of value to emphasize the *theoretical* importance of your study in advancing the state of knowledge in your specific area of research.

STAGE V: Statement of Value
Theoretical Orientation

EXAMPLE A: Both of the factors under investigation in this study *may be of importance in explaining* the irregular occurrence of this disease.

EXAMPLE B: Results of this study *may suggest a broader hypothesis for further research* into the effects of atmospheric chemicals on rubber.

EXERCISE 4.3 Analysis

Do the following tasks.

1. Look back at the introduction about the food buying habits of student wives at the beginning of the chapter. Indicate the sentence that contains Stage V.

   Sentence _____

2. Look back at the introduction about business and financial risk in Exercise 4.1. Is there a Stage V included in this introduction?

   Yes _____ No _____

3. Sometimes Stage V is combined with Stage IV in the same sentence. In each of the following sentences, draw a slash (/) to indicate where Stage IV (the statement of purpose) ends, and Stage V (the statement of value) begins.

   ⎯⎯⎯⎯⎯⎯⎯⎯⎯⎯⎯⎯⎯⎯⎯⎯

   a. This paper describes some demographic factors that might be important for a better understanding of rural-to-urban migration in developing countries.

   b. The aim of this investigation was to study groundwater conditions in order to aid in evaluating the general hydrologic situation in the area under study.

   c. The purpose of this study was to learn more about the food-buying habits of student wives so that areas of weakness or lack of knowledge could be exposed to those who are responsible for planning courses and programs in consumer education.

   d. The effect of soil temperature on Verticillium wilt disease in peppers is discussed in this paper, as is varietal susceptibility of the pepper host, both of which may be of importance in explaining the irregular occurrence of the disease in California.

   ⎯⎯⎯⎯⎯⎯⎯⎯⎯⎯⎯⎯⎯⎯⎯⎯

EXERCISE 4.4   Identification/Arrangement

The following sentences are taken from an introduction to a research report in the field of environmental engineering. Identify the stage that each sentence represents (from I to IV), and then number the sentences in the order you believe the authors used when they wrote the report. You may find more than one sentence for each stage.

UPGRADING LAGOON EFFLUENTS WITH ROCK FILTERS

a. _____ Very simply, a rock filter consists of a submerged bed of rocks through which the lagoon effluent is passed horizontally (1).

b. _____ However, previous research on rock filters has not fully identified the basic algal removal mechanism or developed a rational design method based on this mechanism.

c. _____ Aerobic stabilization lagoons are commonly employed by small cities and isolated industrial plants for wastewater treatment.

d. _____ The objective of this project was to confirm that sedimentation is the primary removal mechanism operating within rock filters.

e. _____ To remove algae from lagoon effluents, a variety of techniques has been proposed including microstraining (2) and chemical coagulation and sedimentation (9).

f. _____ An additional promising alternative for the removal of algae from lagoon effluents is the rock filter (6, 7, 8, 11, 12).

EXERCISE 4.5   Library

Find the introduction to a study in your field from a thesis, dissertation, or journal article in your library. Identify Stages III, IV, and V. Also, indicate:

1. which orientation (*research* or *report*) the author used in Stage IV;
2. which point of view (*practical* or *theoretical*) the author used in Stage V;
3. what *research question* the author(s) had in mind when they designed the study.

LANGUAGE CONVENTIONS

Signal Words and Verb Tenses in Stages III, IV, and V

As we have seen, when you write each of the last three stages to your introduction, you have several choices in determining the kind of focus you wish to give to your information. The choices you make in each case will determine the vocabulary and grammatical structures you will need in order to write these stages.

SEE WHAT YOU ALREADY KNOW   Pretest

The following introduction is taken from the field of agribusiness. It discusses the problem of making good decisions in selecting farm machinery. Fill in each blank space with any appropriate word.

MACHINERY SELECTION MODELING:
INCORPORATION OF WEATHER VARIABILITY

[1]The machinery selection decision confronting agricultural producers is recurrent, complex, and important. [2]Machinery selection is complicated by many interrelated factors which jointly determine the final impact of a particular machinery decision on

farm profitability. **3**Among the more important factors that must be considered in the selection of machinery are (a) weather conditions, (b) the effect of timeliness of operation on yield, (c) availability of labor at crucial times of the year, and (d) the farmer's goals and attitudes toward risk. **4**The interaction among all these factors has a considerable influence on crop planning and machinery selection, and therefore these two decisions must be considered simultaneously.

5The importance and complexity of the machinery selection problem has resulted in numerous efforts to develop analytical models which will either yield generalizable selection guidelines or be useful directly by the farmer as a decision aid. **6**The approaches that have been used are (a) calculator-type programs (17); (b) simulations (3, 10); and (c) mathematical programming approaches (4, 11). **7**To date, many sophisticated models have been developed. **8** _____, to the authors' knowledge, only linear programming approaches have had extensive application and farmer use (2).

9This paper _____ an attempt to develop an alternative analytical approach to machinery selection problems. **10**This alternative approach _____ provide agricultural advisors with a reliable means to help farmers make good decisions in selecting their machinery.

Stage III: Signal Words

Special signal words are commonly used to indicate the beginning of Stage III. Connectors such as *however* are used for this purpose. The connector is followed immediately by a *gap statement* in the present or present perfect tense, which often contains modifiers such as *few*, *little*, or *no*.

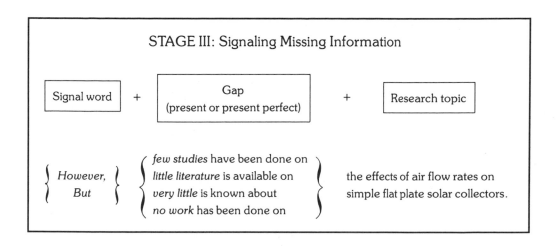

Subordinating conjunctions like *although* and *while* can also be used to signal Stage III. If you use these kinds of signals, you must write a complex sentence, using modifiers like *some, many,* or *much* in the first clause, and modifiers like *little, few,* or *no* in the second clause.

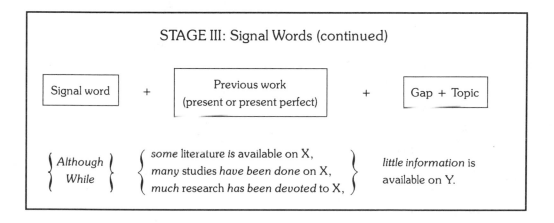

Notice that nouns like *literature, research,* and *work* are uncountable and are therefore followed by *singular* verb forms.

EXERCISE 4.6   Fill-in

The next two excerpts are taken from different introductions, and each contains an example of Stage III. Fill in each blank space with an appropriate signal word.

A. THE EFFECT OF MICROCOMPUTER-ASSISTED
INSTRUCTION ON THE
COMPUTER LITERACY OF FIFTH GRADE STUDENTS

... Thus, the research literature suggests that computer assisted instruction (CAI) is somewhat more effective than conventional instruction in promoting student achievement, improving student attitudes, and decreasing the amount of time needed for instruction. _____, there is very _____ research that reveals how CAI affects students' knowledge or feelings about computers.

B. SOME CHEMICAL EFFECTS IN FATIGUE
CRACKING OF VULCANIZED RUBBER

... A recent study (1) of the failure of rubber strips due to repeated stretching has indicated that the process is caused by gradual tearing. The tear begins as a small flaw and then gradually increases until catastrophic failure occurs. This simple theory is remarkably successful in predicting the fatigue life of strips of soft vulcanized rubber (1,2). _____ there is some evidence that chemical processes may also contribute to rubber fatigue, there is _____ literature available concerning this possibility.

Stage IV: Orientation and Tense

We have already seen that Stage IV, the statement of purpose, can be written from either of two points of view, a *research* or a *report* orientation. If you choose the research orientation you should use the *past tense*, because the research activity has already been completed.

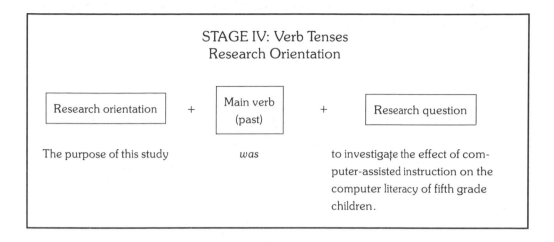

STAGE IV: Verb Tenses
Research Orientation

| Research orientation | + | Main verb (past) | + | Research question |

The purpose of this study — *was* — to investigate the effect of computer-assisted instruction on the computer literacy of fifth grade children.

On the other hand, if you choose to use the *report* orientation, use the *present* or *future* tense.

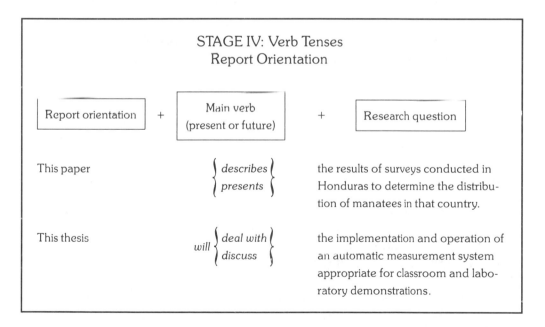

STAGE IV: Verb Tenses
Report Orientation

| Report orientation | + | Main verb (present or future) | + | Research question |

This paper — { *describes* / *presents* } — the results of surveys conducted in Honduras to determine the distribution of manatees in that country.

This thesis — *will* { *deal with* / *discuss* } — the implementation and operation of an automatic measurement system appropriate for classroom and laboratory demonstrations.

Notice that in both research as well as report orientation, phrases like *this study* and *the present paper* reinforce the fact that Stage IV refers to your work, not the work of the other authors mentioned earlier.

EXERCISE 4.7 Transformation

Rewrite each of the Stage IV statements given here, changing the orientation from *research* to *report*, or vice versa. Make any necessary changes in word choice and verb tense.

1. This thesis develops and explains a digital computer simulation capable of accompanying both symmetrical and asymmetrical mutual coupling between parallel circuits.

2. The aim of this investigation was to study the groundwater conditions in the closed Animas Basin to aid in evaluating the hydrologic conditions of the area.

3. The experiment to be described below was an attempt to provide some further data on the role and position of a summary in a research report, using natural materials.

4. The purpose of this research was to further investigate and characterize the Sanitary Engineering Research Laboratory reactor system.

5. This paper will discuss some demographic factors which might be important for queen rearing in African honeybee colonies.

Stage IV and Your Research Question

Your statement of purpose (Stage IV) should be directly related to the research question upon which you based your study. Although you may not need to include the research question *explicitly* in your report, the statement of purpose should be written so that your reader can *infer* the research question behind your study.

If the implied research question is a *yes* or *no* question, the connecting words *whether* or *if* are used in Stage IV, and a modal auxiliary like *would* or *could* accompanies the verb.

```
┌──────────────────────────────────────────────────────────────────────┐
│                                                                        │
│        STAGE IV: Implied Questions in the Statement of Purpose         │
│                                                                        │
│                     Yes or No Questions                                │
│                                                                        │
│                                                                        │
│        ┌─────────────────────┐       ┌──────────────────────────┐      │
│        │  Research question  │       │  Purpose (implied question) │    │
│        └─────────────────────┘       └──────────────────────────┘      │
│                                                                        │
│    Is an automatic measurement system      The purpose of this thesis is to determine │
│    suitable for classroom and laboratory    if an automatic measurement system  │
│    demonstrations?                          would be suitable for classroom and  │
│                                             laboratory demonstrations.           │
│                                                                        │
└──────────────────────────────────────────────────────────────────────┘
```

When the implied question is an *information question, if/whether* is omitted and an infinitive or noun phrase is used.

```
┌──────────────────────────────────────────────────────────────────────┐
│                                                                        │
│        STAGE IV: Implied Questions in the Statement of Purpose         │
│                                                                        │
│                     Information Questions                              │
│                                                                        │
│                                                                        │
│        ┌─────────────────────┐       ┌──────────────────────────┐      │
│        │  Research question  │       │  Purpose (implied question) │    │
│        └─────────────────────┘       └──────────────────────────┘      │
│                                                                        │
│    What is the distribution and status of   This paper reports the results of surveys │
│    manatees in Honduras?                    and interviews conducted in order to │
│                                             determine the distribution and status of │
│                                             manatees in Honduras.               │
│                                                                        │
│                                             This paper reports on the distribution and │
│                                             status of manatees in Honduras.     │
│                                                                        │
└──────────────────────────────────────────────────────────────────────┘
```

EXERCISE 4.8   Transformation

Here you are given several research questions implying different experimental purposes. Convert each question to a Stage IV statement of purpose. Practice using both report and research orientation.

1. What are the groundwater characteristics of the Animas Basin in Colorado?
2. Do bacteria counts differ under transient and steady-state conditions using the direct microscopic count method?
3. What is the optimal engineering design method for rock filter systems?
4. Can alluvial diamond deposits be analyzed as systematically as any other geological phenomenon?
5. How long does advertising affect the sales of a particular product?

Stage V—Model Auxiliaries and Tentativeness

Stage V, the statement of value, is usually written in a way that suggests an attitude of *tentativeness* or *modesty* on the part of the author. When reporting your own study, you should not sound too sure of the benefits, either practical or theoretical, of your work. It is conventional to sound more cautious. This is accomplished in Stage V by using modal auxiliaries, principally *may*.

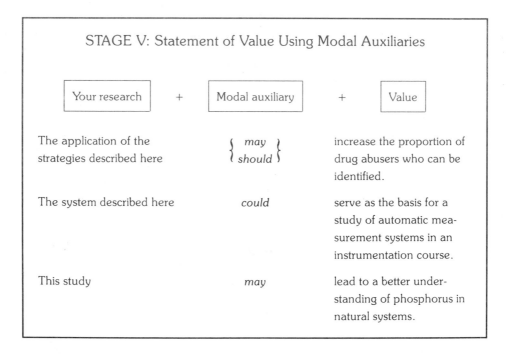

STAGE V: Statement of Value Using Modal Auxiliaries

Your research	+	Modal auxiliary	+	Value
The application of the strategies described here		{ *may* / *should* }		increase the proportion of drug abusers who can be identified.
The system described here		*could*		serve as the basis for a study of automatic measurement systems in an instrumentation course.
This study		*may*		lead to a better understanding of phosphorus in natural systems.

Selecting the Best Modal Auxiliaries for Use in Stages IV and V

Selecting the most appropriate modal auxiliary is often a problem because the meanings of some of these words differ only slightly from one another. Use the chart below to help you choose the best modal auxiliary when you are writing these stages. The modals are listed here in order of their *degree of tentativeness*.

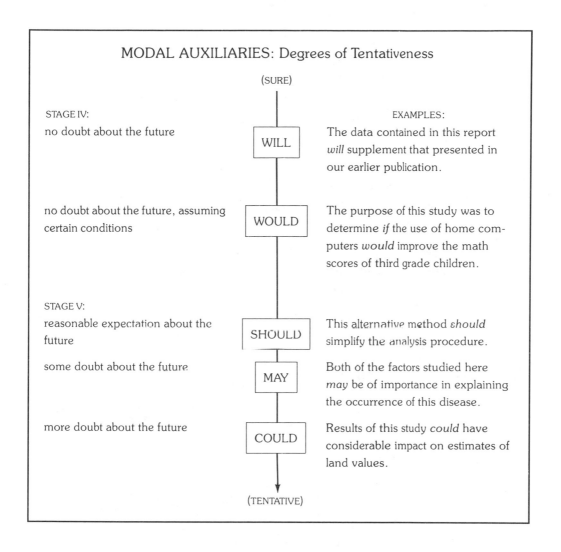

MODAL AUXILIARIES: Degrees of Tentativeness

(SURE)

STAGE IV:
no doubt about the future

WILL

EXAMPLES:
The data contained in this report *will* supplement that presented in our earlier publication.

no doubt about the future, assuming certain conditions

WOULD

The purpose of this study was to determine *if* the use of home computers *would* improve the math scores of third grade children.

STAGE V:
reasonable expectation about the future

SHOULD

This alternative method *should* simplify the analysis procedure.

some doubt about the future

MAY

Both of the factors studied here *may* be of importance in explaining the occurrence of this disease.

more doubt about the future

COULD

Results of this study *could* have considerable impact on estimates of land values.

(TENTATIVE)

EXERCISE 4.9   Fill-in

Fill in an appropriate modal auxiliary in each blank space in the following Stage IV and V statements.

1. The study reported here was made to determine whether solar space-heating and domestic hot-water systems for single-family residences _____ be economically competitive with conventional gas systems.

2. The study reported here examined patterns of health-care use. It attempted to determine if public health education programs for low socioeconomic level consumers _____ result in increased use of the service.

3. The purpose of this study was to learn more about the food buying practices of university student wives so that areas of weakness or lack of knowledge _____ be exposed to those who are responsible for planning course work and programs in consumer education.

4. This report compiles the history of locally owned retail clothing stores in the Southwest. The perspectives of the successes and failures in this retail sector _____ be of use to those who are considering entering the market in this area.

EXERCISE 4.10   Identification

The following excerpt is the final paragraph of an introduction to a thesis in the field of computer science. Underline the <u>verbs</u>, <u>modal auxiliaries</u>, and <u>signal word</u> in Stages III, IV, and V, and notice the degree of tentativeness of each modal auxiliary.

PROGRAMMABLE MEASUREMENT FOR
USE IN AN EDUCATIONAL ENVIRONMENT

[1]The advantages of an automatic measurement system over manual methods of collecting and analyzing data should be apparent to

anyone who has used manual methods of collecting and analyzing data. **2**However, the superiority of automatic analysis has not yet been demonstrated in an educational environment. **3**The greatest realization of these advantages comes when the two methods are compared side by side. **4**It is the purpose of this thesis to outline the implementation and use of an automatic measurement system for classroom use. **5**This is done with the hope that it may provide an alternative solution to the problem of manually demonstrating principles and theories in an educational environment. **6**Additionally, the system may serve as a basis for the study of automatic measurement systems in an instrumentation course. **7**The simplicity of implementation and operation should enable the student to observe details required in all systems without the usual problem of having to learn complex operating and programming procedures.

EXERCISE 4.11   Fill-in

The introduction paragraph about computers in the classroom is given here again. This time, without looking back at the original, fill in each blank with an appropriate *verb*, *modal auxiliary*, or *signal word*.

1The advantages of an automatic measurement system over manual methods of collecting and analyzing data should be apparent to anyone who has used manual methods of collecting and analyzing data. **2**_____, the superiority of automatic analysis _____ not yet been demonstrated in an educational environment. **3**The greatest realization of these advantages comes when the two methods are compared side by side. **4**It _____ the purpose of this thesis to outline the implementation and use of an automatic measurement system for classroom use. **5**This is done with the hope that it _____ provide an alternative solution to the problem of manually demonstrating principles and theories in an educational environment. **6**Additionally, the system _____ serve as a basis for the study of automatic measurement systems in an instrumentation course. **7**The simplicity of implementation and operation _____ enable the student to observe details required in all systems without the usual problem of having to learn complex operating and programming procedures.

EXERCISE 4.12   Reconstruction

The same introduction you have been practicing with is again given here, but this time the sentences are indicated only by lists of key words. Without referring to the original, reconstruct one sentence from each list. Add all necessary words and word endings, and write out each group as a complete sentence. The key words are grouped and listed in the correct order.

---

1. advantages
   automatic measurement
      system
   apparent
   anyone
   use manual methods
   collect, analyze data

2. superiority
   automatic analysis
   not demonstrate
   educational environment

3. purpose
   this thesis
   outline
   implementation, use
   automatic measurement
      system
   classroom use

4. done
   hope
   provide alternative solution
   problem
   manually demonstrating
   principles, theories
   educational environment

5. simplicity
   operation, implementation
   enable student
   observe details
   without
   learn complex operating,
      programming proce-
      dures

EXERCISE 4.13   Library

Using the same sample introduction you obtained for Library Exercise 4.1, do the following tasks.

1. Identify the verb tenses, modal auxiliaries, and signal words used by the writer(s) in Stages III, IV, and V of the introduction.
2. Determine if the author's choice of tense and modals in your example follows the rules you have learned here.
3. Explain why the writer chose these particular tenses and modal auxiliaries.

INTEGRATION

EXERCISE 4.14   Guided Writing

Following is the introduction to a research report in the field of psychology. The Abstract, Stage I, II, and the first part of III are given in their original form. The rest of Stages III, IV, and V are given in outline form. Using the information in the outline, complete the introduction by writing out Stages III, IV, and V.

***

FIFTY CENTURIES OF RIGHT-HANDEDNESS:
THE HISTORICAL RECORD

Abstract. A historical survey of more than 5000 years of art works, including 1180 examples of paintings and drawings showing humans using tools or weapons, revealed no systematic trends in hand usage. The right hand was used in an average of 93% of the cases, regardless of which historical period or geographical region was examined.

Stage I   It is common knowledge that contemporary man prefers to use his right hand when performing tasks requiring one hand. Basically, there are two types of theories that attempt to explain the development of right hand preference in man. The first maintains that there

Stage II   are physiological predispositions, possibly inherited, which lead to the preference of one hand over the other (1). The second type of theory suggests that social or environmental pressures (or both) lead to the high incidence of right hand preference in man (3). This

	theory is supported by human and animal studies that have attempted to alter hand preference through behavioral manipulation (4).
Stage III	Unfortunately, these theories are difficult to test since written references to the distribution of hand preferences throughout history are rare. There are, however, other sources which can be used to investigate historical trends in the distribution of hand preference. Nearly all cultures have art forms that depict human beings engaged in various activities. We might expect that such drawings and paintings would imitate the distribution of hand use that the artist actually observed in his culture.

Stage III (continued)	This possibility: already suggested (5) no systematic studies yet
Stage IV	This study: 1. examine works of art—various cultures —various periods of history 2. describe history of hand preference, 5000 years

Stage V	May clarify:
	two theories of hand preference—which valid?
	            —physiological theory
	            —social pressure theory

EXERCISE 4.15 Writing Up Your Own Research

Look back at the introductory material you wrote in Chapters 2 and 3 for the individual or group study that you chose earlier in this book. In those chapters you wrote a Stage I and II for the introduction to your study. Now, complete your introduction by adding Stages III, IV, and V. As you write each of these stages, remember to:

1. sum up the literature review by including a statement indicating a *gap* in the work of other authors (Stage III);
2. clearly announce the *objective(s)* of your own study in a statement of purpose (Stage IV);
3. claim some *value* for carrying out your study, either on practical or theoretical grounds, or both (Stage V).

When you finish writing these stages, put them together with Stages I and II of your introduction. You may want to make some changes so that each stage leads smoothly and logically to the next. There should be a direct and obvious relationship between each of the five stages and the next.

NOTE: Although the introduction appears first in the report, many researchers carry out their studies and consider their results before writing this section.

CHECKLIST FOR CHAPTER 4

Introduction: Stages III, IV, and V

INFORMATION

_____ Include all three stages in their proper order.

_____ Indicate a gap in the research in Stage III.

_____ Choose research or report orientation for Stage IV.

_____ Choose theoretical or applied perspective for Stage V.

LANGUAGE

_____ Use appropriate signal words and modifiers in Stage III.

_____ Use present or past tense in Stage IV, depending on orientation.

_____ Use modal auxiliaries to indicate tentativeness in Stage V.

5

METHOD

OVERVIEW

After the introduction, the second major section of the experimental research report, often labeled **method**, describes the steps you followed in conducting your study and the materials you used at each step. The method section is useful to readers who want to know how the methodology of your study may have influenced your results, or who are interested in replicating or extending your study.

In this chapter we first look at the general kinds of information included in method; then we focus on the part of the method section that describes *procedural steps*. In the next chapter we examine *materials*.

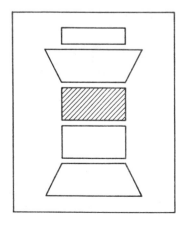

FIGURE 5.1   Method.

INFORMATION CONVENTIONS

The main part of the method section is a description of the *procedural steps* used in your study and the *materials* employed at each step. However, other elements are commonly described in this section as well. In the following example from the field of bilingual education, notice the elements that have been included under method.

AUDITORY COMPREHENSION OF ENGLISH BY MONOLINGUAL AND BILINGUAL PRESCHOOL CHILDREN

Method

overview
: [1]A bilingual group and a monolingual group, each comprised of 30 children, were compared. [2]In each group there were

sample
: six subjects at each of five different age levels. [3]The subjects were selected from seven day care centers in Houston. [4]These centers

restrictions
: accept only children from below poverty threshold; thus, comparable socioeconomic status among the test subjects was insured.

sampling technique
: [5]The bilingual subjects were selected from the 99 Mexican-American children in a previous study (Carrow, 1971) on the basis of performance at age mean or above in both languages on a test of auditory comprehension. [6]This criterion was employed to assure basic understanding of both languages.

materials
: [7]The test instrument employed in this study was a revised version of the Auditory Test for Language Comprehension (Carrow, 1968), which permits the assessment of oral language comprehension of English and Spanish without requiring language expression. [8]It consists of a set of 114 plates, each of which contains three black and white line drawings representing 15 grammatical categories.

procedure
: [9]Both groups were tested by the same examiner, a Mexican-American fluent in both languages. [10]The children were brought individually to a test area where they engaged in spontaneous conversation. [11]For the bilingual children, conversations were conducted in English and Spanish to determine the language in which each child appeared more fluent. [12]Each bilingual subject was tested first in the language in which he demonstrated less fluency so that learning would not be a significant factor in

procedure

subsequent performance when the test was administered again in the second language.

[13]The test required the child to indicate his response by pointing to the picture which corresponded to the examiner's utterance. [14]A score of one was given for each item passed. [15]Test administration required 30 to 45 minutes in each language for each child.

statistical treatment

[16]A 2 × 5 analysis of variance was used to test for age and language group differences.

WHAT HAVE YOU OBSERVED?

1. What elements other than *procedures* and *materials* did the author include in this section?
2. Why do you think the author chose to order the elements in this way?
3. Did you find this procedural description clear and easy to understand?

Ordering your Information

The elements included in the method section and the order in which they are presented are not fixed. However, the list in the following box is conventional and provides you with a good model.

INFORMATION ELEMENTS INCLUDED IN METHOD

Overview of the Experiment
Population/Sample
Location
Restrictions/Limiting Conditions
Sampling Technique
*Procedures
*Materials
Variables
Statistical Treatment

(*always included)

EXERCISE 5.1   Analysis

Read the following example of a method section from the field of wildlife science. The study investigated the blood chemistry of bears and its relationship to seasonal changes in bears' activity. Identify the information elements you find in each sentence of the selection. (NOTE: Some sentences may contain more than one element.)

RATIO OF SERUM UREA TO SERUM CREATININE IN WILD BLACK BEARS

Method

[1]Our 3-year study of changes in the ratio of serum urea to serum creatinine in Colorado wild bears began in the winter of 1981 and ended in the fall of 1983. [2]The investigation was performed in the Black Mesa-Crystal Creek area in west-central Colorado. [3]The study area has three major vegetation bands: a mountain shrub community at lower elevations (2235 to 2330 m), large aspen forests at elevations between 2330 and 3330 m, and mixed forests of Engelmann spruce and fir at higher elevations. [4]A total of 76 blood samples were obtained from 27 female and 21 male bears. [5]Bears were captured with Aldrich spring-activated foot and lower leg snares. [6]Snared bears were immobilized with a combination of ketamine hydrochloride and xylazine hydrochloride. [7]A six-foot pole was used to administer the drug. [8]In winter the bears were located with a radio signal emitted by the bears' collars. [9]The samples were cooled, serum was separated from red blood cells, and urea and creatinine concentrations were determined. [10]Statistical analysis of changes in blood parameters was done with Scheffé's comparison because seasonal values could not be considered either independent or dependent.

Sentence 1: _____   Sentence 6: _____

Sentence 2: _____   Sentence 7: _____

Sentence 3: _____   Sentence 8: _____

Sentence 4: _____   Sentence 9: _____

Sentence 5: _____   Sentence 10: _____

Writing the Procedural Description

The description of the steps you followed in conducting your study should be written clearly so that a reader in your field could accurately replicate your procedure. Of course, the best way to describe a procedure is step-by-step, or *chronologically*.

EXERCISE 5.2   Arrangement

The method section from a research report in the field of medicine is given here with the sentences in scrambled order. Rearrange and number the sentences in a more conventional order, as you think the authors originally wrote them.

MAINTENANCE ENERGY COST OF PREGNANCY AND INFLUENCE OF DIETARY STATUS IN RURAL GAMBIAN WOMEN

Method

a. _____ In other respects the supplemented ten women were similar to the unsupplemented. All received the same clinical and prenatal care.

b. _____ At the time of birth, the weight, head circumference, and gestational age of the babies were assessed as described previously (Lawrence et al., 1983).

c. _____ Twelve women from one of these villages were offered supplementary food 6 days a week. The remaining ten women from the other two villages were unsupplemented.

d. _____ Resting metabolic rate (RMR) and body weight for each woman were measured approximately every 6 weeks during pregnancy. Subjects were asked not to eat or work beforehand. After the subject had lain quietly in an air-conditioned room for 30 min, RMR was measured by open-circuit calorimetry.

e. _____ Twenty-two pregnant women ages 20–32 years from three villages in a remote rural area of Gambia, West Africa, were investigated.

f. _____ The subjects breathed through a respiratory valve and expired air was collected into a Douglas bag. The volume was measured with a large capacity wet-type gas meter (Alexander Wright Co Ltd, London). Oxygen and carbon dioxide concentrations were measured with a Servomex 0A580 oxygen analyser (Taylor Instrument Analytics Ltd, Crowborough, Sussex) and a model SSI carbon dioxide analyser (Analytical Development Co Ltd, Herts).

EXERCISE 5.3 Analysis

Read each of the following sentences, or groups of sentences. They are all taken from method sections of different published studies. In each case, determine which element is represented.

1. _____ The abdomen was closed and the electrodes were connected to two Disa stimulators (Disamatic, Inc.) so that the costal and crural parts could be stimulated separately.

2. _____ The study areas were established on a watershed draining the southeast slopes of Mt. Summerford on the Dona Ana range on the University Ranch, 40 km NNE of Las Cruces, Dona Ana County, New Mexico.

3. _____ Three gibberellic acid combinations, 0, 500, and 1000 ppm, were used in a factorial combination of treatments replicated 10 times in a completely randomized design.

4. _____ The ocean depth in the area under study is 2000 m.

5. _____ The subjects were 116 students of English as a second language enrolled in the Continuing Education Program at Queens College, New York.

6. _____ A proportionate, stratified, random, cross-sectional sample was employed. The number of workers from each trade included in the study reflected the proportion of the construction population represented by that trade.

7. _____ Analyses of variance were used to detect significant differences among varieties or locations. Duncan's multiple range test was used to separate means.

EXERCISE 5.4 Library

In the library find a study in your field (either a journal article, a thesis, or a dissertation). Locate the section or chapter corresponding to method and make a photocopy of the section. Then answer the following questions.

1. Is the section (or chapter) in your report labeled "method"? If not, what is it called?

2. Which of the elements from the list on page 92 can you find in your example? In what order are they presented?

3. Read the part of your example that describes the *procedure* used in the study. Is it written clearly enough so that you can easily understand the sequence of steps that the experimenters describe?

LANGUAGE CONVENTIONS

Choosing Verb Tense and Voice in Procedural Description

Several grammatical conventions govern the method section. In this chapter we concentrate on those conventions governing the *procedural description*. These concern choosing the correct *verb tense* and *verb voice*.

SEE WHAT YOU ALREADY KNOW   Pretest

The following procedural description is taken from a report in the field of civil engineering. It describes a construction project in which a special technique was used in building a dam to stabilize the ground under the structure. Fill in each blank space with any appropriate word.

STABILIZATION OF SOILS BY MEANS OF ELECTRO-OSMOSIS

Procedure

[1]An earthen dam was constructed across the West Branch of the Mahoning River in northeastern Ohio. [2]Three spillway conduits at the base of the dam _____ monitored for deformation during construction of the embankment. [3]Just prior to completion of the embankment, large deformations _____. [4]The top of the embankment _____ subsequently moved, and piezometers were installed. [5]It was _____ that the piezometric levels in the clay were extremely high. [6]Stability analyses _____ that the piezometric levels needed to be immediately lowered, and electro-osmosis was _____ as the most suitable method for this purpose.

[7]Electrodes were positioned at the bottom of the clay deposit, along the central 1000-ft long portion of the embankment. [8]Eight rows of electrodes _____ installed along the top of the embankment, and six rows _____ placed along both the upstream and downstream sides.

9The power was _____ by 14 generators
with capacities ranging from 90 to 300 KW. **10**When fully
operational , the generators _____ about
14,000 amps. **11**The total elapsed time from the beginning to the
end of the treatment _____ about 10 months.

Choosing the Correct Verb Tense in Procedural Descriptions

The procedures you used in carrying out your study should usually be described in the *simple past tense*. Sentences included under method that are not written in the past tense usually do *not* refer to the procedures used in the study being reported. Instead, they may describe standard procedures that are commonly used by others.

PROCEDURAL DESCRIPTIONS:
Past Tense

Surveys *were* sent to student health services at 180 colleges.

The study *was* carried out on a marine laboratory research vessel.

The generators *supplied* about 14,000 amps when fully operational.

NOTE: In a few fields of study, procedural descriptions can sometimes be written in the *simple present tense*. You should check journals in your field (see Exercise 5.11) or ask professors in your university department to determine which convention to use.

EXERCISE 5.5   Analysis

Read the following excerpt and examine Figure 5.2, both taken from another report in the field of civil engineering. This study investigated possible construction designs for the underground stations in a subway system. The excerpt includes much information *not* directly related to the method used in the study. Identify those sentences that specifically deal with the *procedure* used in conducting this study.

SUBWAY CONSTRUCTION COSTS:
THE ROLE OF THE ENGINEER

[1]The determination to locate a route underground is a basic factor in the cost of the fixed facilities of the transit system. [2]Once the decision is made to build underground, the general station locations are selected. [3]Design and construction costs then become controlled by station configuration, site considerations, geotechnical conditions, station size, and system depth. [4]These factors indicate the large potential range of construction costs for underground subway stations. [5]To illustrate this range, several transit systems were visited, and seven typical station designs were developed as a representative range of acceptable solutions (see Figure 5.2).

[6]The first five types are open cut, and the last two are mined. [7]Types 1 and 2 are very shallow or at platform level. [8]Stations such as those are common to most systems, and particularly to Mexico City. [9]Type 3 is a low-height train room with the mezzanine underground, separated from the main train room. [10]The Toronto stations are examples of this type. [11]Type 4 is a station with platforms stacked one above the other. [12]Although this station is not often used, it has advantages in narrow or constricted areas. [13]Type 5 is a station with the mezzanine inside the train room. [14]Many systems are adopting this type of station. [15]Type 6 is a single-chamber system, and Type 7 is constructed with multiple chambers. [16]Type 6 is not widely used, but Type 7 is used extensively, e.g., in London.

[17]Cost estimates were prepared for these various stations at different depths of cover, assuming that ground conditions, utilities, adjacent structures, and other controls were constant over the range of estimates. [18]In order to standardize estimates and permit comparison of cost factors, station Type 5 was used as the reference station. [19]The cost for this station with 20 ft of cover was calculated and established at 1.00—the basis for comparative estimates.

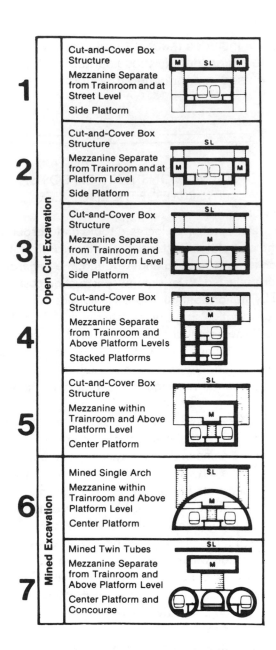

1 Cut-and-Cover Box Structure

Mezzanine Separate from Trainroom and at Street Level

Side Platform

2 Cut-and-Cover Box Structure

Mezzanine Separate from Trainroom and at Platform Level

Side Platform

3 Cut-and-Cover Box Structure

Mezzanine Separate from Trainroom and Above Platform Level

Side Platform

4 Cut-and-Cover Box Structure

Mezzanine Separate from Trainroom and Above Platform Levels

Stacked Platforms

5 Cut-and-Cover Box Structure

Mezzanine within Trainroom and Above Platform Level

Center Platform

6 Mined Single Arch

Mezzanine within Trainroom and Above Platform Level

Center Platform

7 Mined Twin Tubes

Mezzanine Separate from Trainroom and Above Platform Level

Center Platform and Concourse

Open Cut Excavation (1–5)

Mined Excavation (6–7)

FIGURE 5.2   Subway station types.

Sentences describing *procedure:* _____, _____, _____, _____.

Choosing the Appropriate Verb Voice—Active or Passive

You can use either the *active* or the *passive voice* when you describe the procedure used in your project. Examples of both voices are given in the following box. Notice that the formation of the passive voice requires the *be* auxiliary + the past participle of a verb.

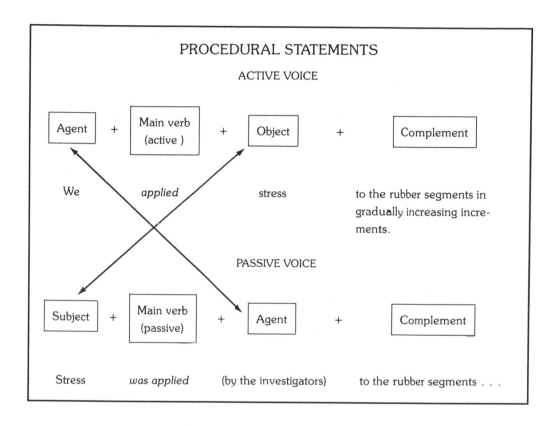

Your decision whether to use the active or passive voice in procedural statements should be made with the following considerations:

1. The passive voice is conventionally used to describe procedure in order to *depersonalize* the information. The passive construction allows you to omit the agent (usually "I" or "we"), placing the emphasis on the procedure and how it was done.

    EXAMPLE A: For reasons related to personal safety, the test facility *was constructed* (by us) in a remote area 4 miles from the main road.

EXAMPLE B: Tests *were conducted* (by me) with four different types of reactors.

However, your professor or editor may specifically ask you *not* to use the passive voice because he or she prefers *a more personal style* with frequent use of the pronouns "I" or "we."

2.   In addition to questions of style, your choice of the active or passive voice should place *old information* near the beginning of the sentence and *new information* at the end. The old information is italicized in each sentence in example C.

EXAMPLE C: The four reactors we tested in the work reported here all contained a platinum catalyst (ACTIVE). Each *reactor-catalyst configuration* will be described separately (PASSIVE). *The quartz reactors* were manufactured by the Wm. A. Sales Company of Wheeling, Illinois (PASSIVE).

EXERCISE 5.6 Transformation

The following methodology description was taken from a report in the field of civil engineering about a highway construction project. It has been altered so that the writers of the report are mentioned as agents in each sentence. Rewrite the description in a *depersonalized* form.

CUT AND COVER CONSTRUCTION ON
UNSTABLE SLOPES

Method

    [1]We started construction of the reinforced concrete structure in July, 1976, and completed it by May, 1977. [2]We built standard sections of forms for the casting of the concrete. [3]We used concrete of the B225 type, in accordance with government regulations. [4]At the two ends of the structure we constructed wingwalls, and we installed three side openings on the downhill side to provide enough daylight to render the use of electric lights unnecessary.

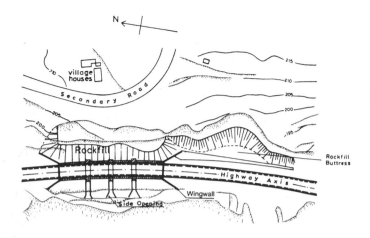

FIGURE 5.3   Reinforced concrete structure.

Using Short Passive Forms to Describe Procedure

In technical and scientific English, there is a tendency to *shorten* certain kinds of passive constructions. Three such kinds of sentences are commonly used in procedural descriptions. The first type is a compound sentence with two identical subjects and two or more verbs in the passive. To shorten this kind of sentence, omit the *subject* and the *be* auxiliary in the second part of the sentence.

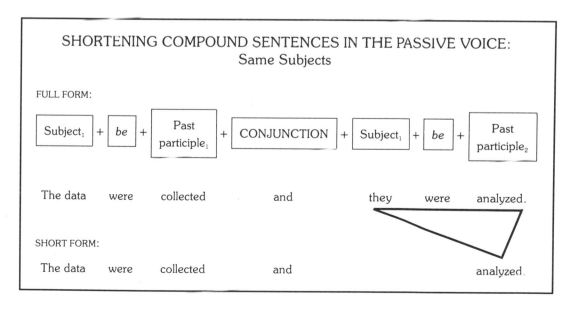

SHORTENING COMPOUND SENTENCES IN THE PASSIVE VOICE:
Same Subjects

FULL FORM:

Subject₁ + be + Past participle₁ + CONJUNCTION + Subject₁ + be + Past participle₂

The data   were   collected   and   they   were   analyzed.

SHORT FORM:

The data   were   collected   and   analyzed.

The second type of sentence is also compound, but in this case there are two different subjects, each with different verbs in the passive voice. To shorten this kind of sentence, omit the *be* auxiliary before the second verb.

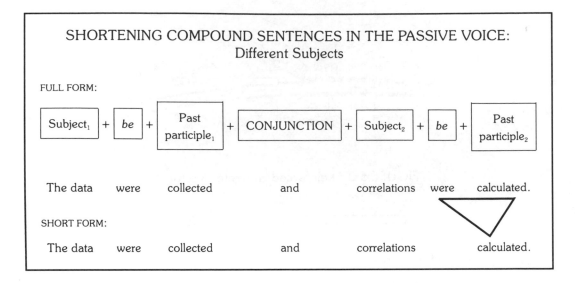

The third type of sentence has a *which* clause containing a passive verb form. In this case, you can shorten the clause by dropping the conjunction *which* and the *be* auxiliary.

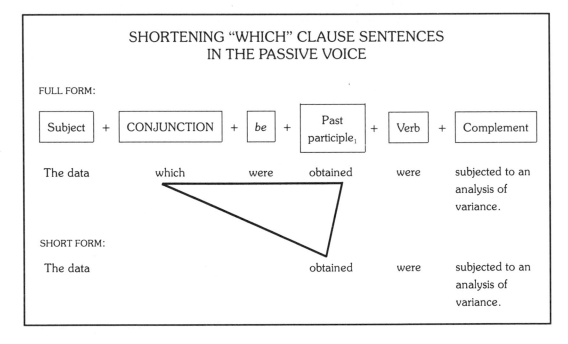

EXERCISE 5.7 Analysis/Transformation

The following sentences are taken from the method section of a report in the field of horticulture. For each example, indicate if the passive voice is used in a *compound sentence* or a *which clause* by writing CS or WC. Then rewrite each sentence in its short form. If no short form is possible, write the abbreviation NSF.

WEED CONTROL IN CHILE PEPPERS AT THE
ESPAÑOLA VALLEY BRANCH STATION

1. _____ Herbicides were applied before planting at various dosage levels to plots consisting of one 30-ft row which was planted on a 36-inch bed.

   _____

2. _____ The preplant treatments were sprayed on the surface of the prepared beds and they were incorporated into the soil by double-discing.

   _____

3. _____ The plants were seeded by hand into the beds to obtain between two to five plants per hill which were spaced at 3-ft intervals.

   _____

4. _____ The variety which was seeded each year was Española No. 1.

   _____

5. _____ A randomized block design was used each year with three replications in 1966 and 1968.

   _____

6. _____ Weed counts were made and records were kept of the time which was required to remove weeds from one 30-ft row.

   _____

EXERCISE 5.8   Identification

Read the following selection describing the procedures used to carry out a study in the field of economics. Underline all examples of the passive voice. Also, underline any short forms of the passive that you recognize.

AN ECONOMIC ANALYSIS OF NATURAL GAS POLICY ALTERNATIVES

Procedures

[1]A mathematical model was developed for the evaluation of alternative natural gas policies. [2]The model is based upon a simplified energy-demand function which relates the quantity of energy consumed to price. [3]This relationship was not estimated by a statistical procedure. [4]Rather, parameters were specified which, on the basis of previous studies, were thought to approximate market behavior.

[5]Energy consumption was defined to include natural gas, oil, and electricity used in the residential, commercial, and industrial sectors. [6]Fuels used for transportation and oil used for industrial feedstock were excluded because natural gas is not generally used for these purposes. [7]It is used to produce anhydrous ammonia, but this was also excluded.

[8]The supply and price of natural gas and the prices of potential natural gas substitutes were specified for each policy option. [9]The model was then used to calculate the price of energy, the quantity of energy, and the quantities of natural gas substitutes that would be consumed. [10]From this information, policy alternatives were evaluated by comparing the consumer expenditure associated with each policy.

EXERCISE 5.9   Fill-in

The procedural description about natural gas policy is given here again. This time, without looking back at the original, fill in each blank space with any appropriate *be* auxiliary or *past participle*.

1A mathematical model _____ developed for the evaluation of alternative natural gas policies. **2**The model is based upon a simplified energy-demand function which relates the quantity of energy consumed to price. **3**This relationship _____ not _____ by a statistical procedure. **4**Rather, parameters _____ specified which, on the basis of previous studies, were _____ to approximate market behavior.

5Energy consumption was defined to include natural gas, oil, and electricity _____ in the residential, commercial, and industrial sectors. **6**Fuels used for transportation and oil _____ for industrial feedstock were _____ because natural gas is not generally used for these purposes. **7**It is used to produce anhydrous ammonia, but this use was also _____.

8The supply and price of natural gas and the prices of potential natural gas substitutes _____ specified for each policy option. **9**The model was then _____ to calculate the price of energy, the quantity of energy, and the quantities of natural gas substitutes that would _____ _____ consumed. **10**From this information, policy alternatives _____ evaluated by comparing the consumer expenditure _____ with each policy.

EXERCISE 5.10 Reconstruction

Part of the procedural section you have been practicing with is given again, but this time the sentences are indicated only by lists of key words. Without looking back to the original, reconstruct one sentence from each list, using *passive voice verbs* or *short passive forms* wherever possible. Add all necessary words and word endings and write out each group as a complete sentence. The key words are grouped and listed in the correct order.

1. mathematical model
   develop
   evaluate
   alternative natural gas
      policies

2. supply, price
   natural gas
   and
   prices
   potential natural gas
      substitutes
   specify
   for each policy option

3. model
   then use
   calculate
   price of energy
   and
   quantities of natural gas
      substitutes
   would be
   consume

4. from this information
   policy alternatives
   evaluate
   compare the cost
   associate
   each

EXERCISE 5.11   Library

Using the same example of experimental procedure that you found for Library Exercise 5.4, answer the following questions.

1. What *verb tense* is used in the description of experimental procedure? Can you find any exceptions to the tense rules we have studied here? If so, can you explain the exceptions?
2. What is the proportion of *active voice verbs* to *passive verbs* in this section? Does this proportion result in a *personalized* or *depersonalized* style of description?
3. What examples of *short passive forms* can you find in your selection?

INTEGRATION

EXERCISE 5.12   Guided Writing

Before he invented the Polaroid Camera, Edwin Land conducted many experiments on color vision and color photography. One of his experiments involved the use of black and white film to produce a color image. This was done with camera filters and projector lamps of different colors. The procedure adapted from one of his experiments is shown here in diagram form. Notice that the procedure consisted of three main steps. Assume that you are Edwin Land and that you are writing a report on this experiment. Using the information contained in the diagram, write the *procedural description*. In order for your description to be clear, you must provide *all* of the pertinent details for each step.

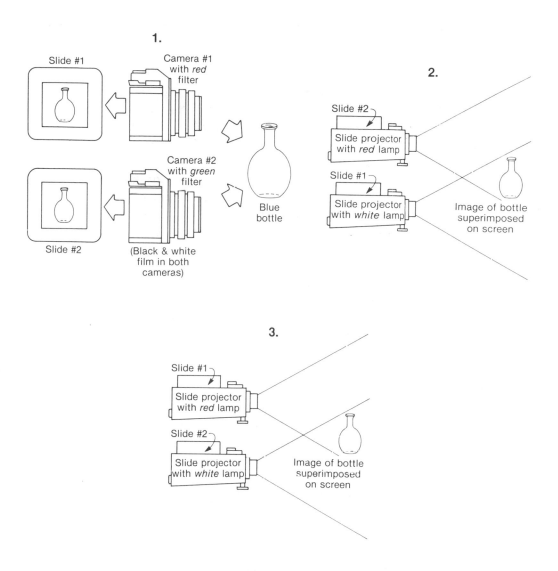

FIGURE 5.4   Color photography experiment.

EXERCISE 5.13   Guided Writing

Following are the introduction and method sections to a study in the field of engineering management. First, read the introduction to the study. Then, from the outline that follows, write a description of the procedures used to carry out the study.

═══════════════════════════════════

VALENCE OF AND SATISFACTION WITH JOB OUTCOMES

Introduction

Job outcomes can be directly related to the experience of performing a task, or they can be allocated by others as a function of performing a task. Outcomes that are directly related to performing a task are termed *intrinsic outcomes*, while those allocated by others are called *extrinsic outcomes*. For example, performing a task that requires the worker to make full use of his/her skills and abilities provides intrinsic outcomes. Pay based upon the quality of one's work qualifies as an extrinsic outcome.

The anticipated satisfaction that one associates with specific job outcomes is a major influence on worker motivation (1). Satisfaction is a function of the job outcomes desired and expected by the worker, and those actually received (2, 3). Workers who receive the outcomes they expect or desire from their work will tend to be satisfied with their work. Satisfied workers exhibit lower absenteeism and file fewer grievances (4). If managers are able to make job satisfaction dependent upon the performance of required tasks, the results should be increased worker motivation and satisfaction.

A study of construction workers was carried out including workers from various trades in the industry to determine how job satisfaction was related to job outcomes among these workers. Results of this study may suggest ways in which construction workers can be motivated to greater productivity by ensuring that they receive the outcomes they expect from their jobs.

Method

Sample — stratified, random, cross-sectional
     — 2800 construction workers, major midwestern city

— different trade unions (carpenters, electricians, plumbers)

— 30 percent of the members of each trade union

Procedure

1. Envelopes — send to local business manager of each union
   — contents: $\begin{cases} \text{cover letter} \\ \text{questionnaire} \\ \text{postage paid return envelope} \end{cases}$

2. Union business manager — request: $\begin{cases} \text{select workers from his union} \\ \text{send envelopes to selected workers} \end{cases}$

3. Workers — fill out questionnaires
   — mail completed questionnaires to investigators (use postage paid return envelopes)

Material

Questionnaire — modified version of Michigan Organizational Assessment Package
   — 703 completed questionnaires returned

Statistical Treatment

Multiple regression—1. measure: overall satisfaction with job
   2. identify: most important job outcomes
   3. correlate: $\begin{cases} \text{job outcomes} \\ \text{job satisfaction} \end{cases}$

EXERCISE 5.14. Writing Up Your Own Research

In previous chapters you have begun writing up an original research project. You have already written the introduction, including a literature review

(Chapters 2, 3, and 4). Now, carry out your study. Plan and follow a series of procedural steps as determined by your purpose and your research design. Develop and use any instruments (such as surveys, questionnaires, tests, and so on) you need in order to collect data. Finally, when you have completed all the steps and collected all your data, write a *procedural description* of the methodology you used. Before you write, remember:

1. Procedural descriptions are arranged chronologically.
2. The past tense is usually used to indicate the procedures which were used in the study.
3. The passive voice and short forms of some passive constructions are commonly used in this section of the research report.

CHECKLIST FOR CHAPTER 5

Describing Experimental Procedure

INFORMATION

_____ Include all information necessary for someone to replicate your procedure.

_____ Describe the procedure chronologically.

LANGUAGE

_____ Use the past tense to describe procedure.

_____ Use the passive voice to depersonalize procedural descriptions and to keep old information at the beginning of sentences.

_____ Use short forms of the passive voice to reduce compound sentences and *which* clauses.

MATERIALS

OVERVIEW

Although the second major section of the experimental research report is often called "method," it is sometimes titled **materials and method**. This combined title indicates that researchers generally describe these two aspects *together* when they write up their research. That is, they simultaneously describe any equipment or other *materials* they used with each step in their procedure. In this chapter we examine materials description in detail and learn how to integrate it with the procedural description.

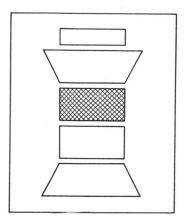

FIGURE 6.1 **Experimental materials.**

INFORMATION CONVENTIONS

By materials we mean any items used to carry out a research project. They may fall into any of the following categories:

MATERIALS

laboratory equipment
field equipment
human or animal subjects
natural substances
fabricated materials
surveys, questionnaires and tests
computer models
mathematical models

Read the following selection taken from a report in the field of solar technology which describes a design for a solar food dryer. Notice the types of information the writer has included in this materials description, and the order in which the information is presented.

A SEE-SAW DRYER

overview

[1]The see-saw dryer was developed for the drying of coffee and cocoa beans. [2]It was intended for small-scale drying operations and could be easily operated. [3]It was designed for use in tropical regions.
    [4]The dryer was operated in two positions along a central axis of rotation running north-south. [5]This see-saw operation permitted the drying material to face the sun more directly during both morning and afternoon.

principal parts

[6]The dryer consisted of a rectangular wood frame divided lengthwise into parallel channels of equal width, and crosswise by means of retaining bars. [7]The bottom of the dryer was made of bamboo matting painted black. [8]The cover of the frame was made

of a film of transparent Polyvinyl Chloride (P.V.C.) which provided a screening effect against ultra violet light, thus reducing photo-degradation of the drying product. [9]All of the internal parts of the dryer were coated with a flat black paint. [10]The drying frame was

function

tilted during operation so that it faced east during the morning and west during the afternoon.

FIGURE 6.2   Solar food dryer.

WHAT HAVE YOU OBSERVED?

1. In what sentence does the physical description of the dryer begin?
2. What is the function of the sentences before that sentence?
3. What type of material is described in this example, based on the categories listed in the previous box?

Ordering Your Information

If the materials you used are well known to researchers in your field, it is conventional to identify them only. However, if you used *specially designed* or unconventional materials in your experiment, it is common to write a detailed description of them in the report. In this case, you should include the following information, in the order given:

DESCRIBING SPECIALLY DESIGNED MATERIALS: Three Steps

A. *Overview:* This step consists of one or two sentences that give a general idea of the material and the purpose for which it is intended.

B. *Description of principal parts:* Here, each major part or characteristic of the material is described in logical sequence.

C. *Functional description:* This last step shows how the various features described in Step B function together.

EXERCISE 6.1   Analysis

Read the following materials section from an article in the field of soil science. It describes a piece of field equipment used to simulate natural rainfall. Identify Steps A, B, and C in the selection (see previous box).

A PORTABLE RAINFALL SIMULATOR
AND RUNOFF SAMPLER

[1]The device described here applies water to an approximately 16 × 20 foot area with kinetic energy approximating that of natural rainfall. [2]It samples and records the rates of runoff in such a way that sediment production can also be measured accurately. [3]Maximum error of 1% in application and in runoff measurements was a goal in the design, as were ease of assembly and transport. [4]The apparatus is patterned partly on that described by Meyer and McCune (2), but it is simpler and more easily transported. [5]The major components (Figure 6.3, top) consist of: 1) a 1500-gallon tank truck for transporting water, and (2) a framework and moving spray assembly for applying water, and (3) a device for

sampling and measuring the rate of runoff. [6]Power is supplied by a 10-horsepower gasoline engine which drives both a centrifugal pump and 2-kw electrical generator. [7]Water from the tank truck is supplied to the apparatus by the centrifugal pump (Homart 736.25). [8]The pressure of the output from the pump is controlled by an adjustable bypass pressure regulator valve plumbed to return the excess water to the tank. [9]The output from the regulator is connected to the spray assembly by 100 feet of 3/4-inch hose. [10]This moving spray assembly applies water to the plots through eight nozzles (Spraying Systems 80100), mounted as specified by Meyer and McCune (2). [11]The assembly is moved back and forth along aluminum I-beams by 1/2-inch roller chains (see Figure 6.4).

FIGURE 6.3   Rainfall simulator.

FIGURE 6.4 Spray assembly.

Step A. *Overview*: From sentence _____ to sentence _____
Step B. *Description of principal parts*: From sentence _____
        to sentence _____
Step C. *Functional description*: From sentence _____ to sentence _____

Ordering the Description of Principal Parts—Step B

In Step B you describe the principal features of the material used in your study. There are two main organizing plans that you can use in this step, depending on your material.

ARRANGEMENT PLANS FOR DESCRIBING PRINCIPAL PARTS
OF MATERIALS (STEP B)

1. *Spatial arrangement:* Describe the features from top to bottom, front to back, left to right, from the center to the outside, or in some other spatial way. This arrangement is especially useful for describing equipment consisting of various connected parts.

2. *Functional arrangement:* Describe the principal features in the order in which they function, from beginning to end. This arrangement is best for describing parts that operate in a fixed sequence.

EXERCISE 6.2 Analysis

Read the following method section from a study about international students in an intensive English program. Then indicate where the description of materials begins. Finally, find Step B (the description of principal parts) and determine what type of arrangement plan is used, *spatial* or *functional*.

DIFFERENTIAL GAIN RATES IN INTENSIVE ESL PROGRAMS

Method

[1]The study employed a pre- and posttest design. [2]The Michigan Test of English Language Proficiency (MTELP) was administered to the students once at the beginning of the program and again 10 months later at the end of the academic year. [3]The MTELP is a standardized measure designed to predict academic success of international students at American colleges and universities. [4]The test consists of 100 items and is divided into three parts. [5]Part I contains 40 questions on grammar; Part II contains 40 questions on vocabulary; and Part III contains 20 questions testing reading comprehension.

[6]Students were given an alternative form of the test at the second administration (posttest). [7]The sample was stratified into three general proficiency groups based on the pretest scores, which we labeled Low, Middle and High. [8]Each group consisted of 21 students, the Low group including students with initial scores of 45 and below, the Middle group with scores falling between 46 and 55, and the High group including pretest scores of 56 and above.

---

1. The materials description begins with sentence _____.

2. Step B (description of principal parts) includes sentences _____ and
    _____.

3. The arrangement plan of Step B is _____.

Integrating Materials with Procedure

The materials used in a study are sometimes described *separately* from the procedures. This arrangement may be used when several different pieces of conventional laboratory equipment are used to carry out a routine procedure. This can be seen in the following example from the field of chemistry.

A.

All the aromatic compounds used were commercially available materials without further purification. 2-propanol was distilled from sodium metal. The instrumentation used included an HFT-80 and NT-300 spectrometer, a Hewlett Packard 5980-A mass spectrometer, a Waters Associates HPLC Instrument, Model 600A, and a Varian Aerograph 1400 GC instrument with a 10-ft column containing 15% Carbowax on Chromosorb W.

More commonly, however, materials and methods are described in an *integrated* form, often with both elements mentioned in each sentence. Notice this arrangement in the following section from the same chemistry experiment. (The _material_ mentioned in each sentence is underlined, and the procedure is ⟨circled.⟩)

B.

[1]Aqueous sodium hydroxide (30 g, 185 mL) ⟨was cooled⟩ in ice in a 500-mL beaker, ⟨stirred magnetically⟩ while 5 g of nickel-aluminum alloy ⟨was added⟩ in several small portions, and gradually ⟨warmed⟩ to 100°C as required to maintain the hydrogen evolution. [2]The nickel ⟨was then allowed to settle,⟩ and the liquid ⟨was decanted.⟩ [3]After ⟨being washed⟩ with 5% fresh sodium hydroxide and distilled water until neutral, the nickel suspension ⟨was filtered⟩ with a glass funnel and then finally ⟨washed⟩ with 100 mL of 2-propanol. [4]The catalyst ⟨was transferred⟩ with small amounts of dry 2-propanol to a glass-stoppered bottle.

EXERCISE 6.3 Analysis

The method section given here is taken from a report in the field of marine geology. It is written in *integrated form*—that is, the materials are described together with the procedure, step by step, in each sentence. After you read the selection, fill in the blanks in each column to indicate each procedural step and the material used in that step.

ALUMINUM IN SEAWATER: CONTROL BY BIOLOGICAL ACTIVITY

Procedures

[1]To investigate seasonal and annual variations in physical, chemical and biological properties of a portion of the Mediterranean Sea, a standard oceanographic station location 12 nautical miles (22 km) west of Calvi, Corsica, has been occupied by the Stareso Marine Laboratory research ship *Recteur Debuission* at irregular intervals since 1974. [2]The ocean depth is 2000 m. [3]Water samples for aluminum (Al) and nutrient analysis were collected there from various depths. [4]Temperature of the samples was determined by reversing thermometers.

[5]All the samples for Al and nutrient analysis were filtered through 0.45-μm Millipore filters immediately after collection. [6]The filtered samples were kept at 4°C in polyethylene bottles for later analysis. [7]To prevent further biological activity, one or two drops of chloroform was added to each sample. [8]The samples were analyzed for Al 2 weeks after collection, using lumogallion as the chelating agent.

PROCEDURAL STEPS	MATERIALS
1. collect water samples	1. from research ship
2. determine temperature	2. reversing thermometers
3. _____	3. _____
4. _____	4. _____
5. _____	5. _____
6. _____	6. _____

LIBRARY EXERCISE 6.4

In the library find a study in your field (a journal article, a thesis, or a dissertation written by a student in your field). Locate the section of the report that describes the materials used in the study. Make a photocopy of this section and then do the following tasks.

1. Identify the *materials* used in the study.
2. Determine whether each material mentioned is *conventional* or *specially designed*.
3. If any of the materials are given an extensive description, find the sentences in the descriptions that correspond to Step A *(overview)*, Step B *(description of principal parts)*, and Step C *(functional description)*.
4. If there is a step B, identify the arrangement as *spatial, functional*, or some other arrangement plan.
5. Determine whether the procedures and materials in your selection are described in an *integrated* form or *separately.*

LANGUAGE CONVENTIONS

Choosing Verb Tense and Voice in Describing Materials

In the first part of this chapter we looked at some conventions for organizing information about the materials used in your study. There are also some grammatical conventions you should know in order to describe materials clearly in your report. These conventions mainly involve choosing the correct *verb tense* and *voice*.

SEE WHAT YOU ALREADY KNOW   Pretest

The following method section is taken from a report in the field of psychiatry. It deals with the potential risk for alcoholism in the children of alcoholic fathers. The subjects are described in this section. Fill in each blank space with any appropriate word.

EVENT-RELATED BRAIN POTENTIALS IN BOYS
AT RISK FOR ALCOHOLISM

Method

[1]Twenty-five sons of alcoholic fathers were tested. [2]The boys
_____ between the ages of 7 and 13, and _____ a
mean age of 11.9 (standard deviation, 2.1). [3]In each case the
father _____ diagnosed as alcoholic and at
one time or another had been treated for alcoholism. [4]We
excluded the boys whose mothers _____ alcoholic, who had
been alcoholic during pregnancy or who _____
excessively after giving birth. [5]Only boys without medical
problems and without exposure to alcohol or
other substances of abuse _____ _____
in this study.

[6]The 25 normal control (NC) subjects were boys who were
matched for socio-economic status and age to the high-risk (HR)
subjects. [7]The NC group _____ a mean age of 12.5 years
(standard deviation, 2.4) and _____ not differ significantly
in age from the HR group. [8]They were _____
in the study only if they had no exposure to alcohol or substances
of abuse, and _____ no history of alcoholism or other
psychiatric disorder in first- or second-degree relatives. [9]All
subjects _____ paid volunteers.

Choosing Verb Tenses—Samples and Populations

Sentences describing the subjects or materials used in a study require either the
past or the *present* tense. Notice that the boys described in the preceding example *were* specific individuals selected to take part in the study. In other words,

they were a *sample* selected by the experimenters to represent an entire population of high risk boys. When we describe the sample used in a study we commonly use the *past tense*.

DESCRIBING SAMPLES: Past Tense Verbs

Sample	Main verb (past)	Description
The boys	were	between the ages of 7 and 13.
The men interviewed	were	primarily from St. Louis, Mo.
The subjects	were	18 Arabic-speaking students attending classes at the American University in Cairo.

However, when describing the *general population* from which the sample subjects were selected, the *present tense* is normally used.

DESCRIBING POPULATIONS: Present Tense Verbs

Population	Main verb (present)	Description
All students who apply for admission to the American University of Cairo	take	the Michigan Test of English Language Proficiency.
They	enter	the English Language Institute where they follow an intensive program of English language training.

EXERCISE 6.5   Fill-in

The following excerpt is taken from a study about the English-language proficiency of university students in Cairo, Egypt. In each blank space, add an appropriate verb in the past or present tense, depending on whether the *sample* or the larger *population* is being described.

INVESTIGATING THE LINGUISTIC ACCEPTABILITY OF EGYPTIAN EFL STUDENTS

Method

[1]The Michigan Test scores of the 18 students in our sample ranged from 71–77%, thus placing them in the upper level English courses. [2]Students in this range of scores generally _____ English skills adequate for communicative purposes, but they still _____ serious mistakes with tenses, articles, prepositions, and word order. [3]These 18 students _____ to us from semi-private Language Schools, where the medium of instruction _____ typically either French or English, in addition to Arabic. [4]For most students from these schools, English _____ the second rather than the first foreign language. [5]The 18 students in our study _____ highly motivated, both to remain at the American University of Cairo and to improve their English proficiency.

Use of Tenses with Conventional and Specially Designed Materials

We have seen previously that verb tense can be determined by whether you are describing a general population or a sample selected from a population. We find a similar convention determining verb tenses when we describe other materials. If you use equipment in your study which is *standard* or *conventional* in your field and probably familiar to most other researchers, you should describe it using the *present tense*.

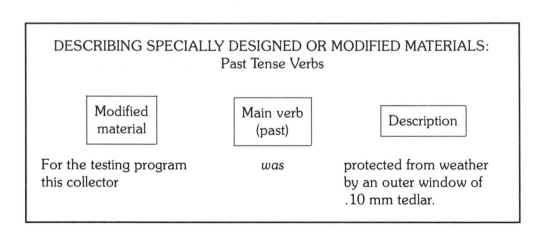

DESCRIBING CONVENTIONAL MATERIAL: Present Tense Verbs

Conventional material	Main verb (present)	Description
The Auditory Test for Language Comprehension (Carrow, 1968)	*permits*	the assessment of oral language comprehension of English and Spanish.
A typical chemical reactor	*includes*	a helical, tube-in-tube heat exchanger.

On the other hand, descriptions of *specially designed* materials with which other workers in your field may not be familiar are usually written in the *past tense*. Common devices that you *modified* in some special way for use in your study are also sometimes described in the past.

DESCRIBING SPECIALLY DESIGNED OR MODIFIED MATERIALS: Past Tense Verbs

Modified material	Main verb (past)	Description
For the testing program this collector	*was*	protected from weather by an outer window of .10 mm tedlar.

EXERCISE 6.6 Identification

Each of the following excerpts comes from a different report. Read each one and determine if the material described is *conventional* (assumed to be familiar to most people in the field) or *specially designed* for the study being reported. Then write C or SD in each blank.

1. _____ The heater consists essentially of a bundle of parallel tubes, the ends of which are expanded into tube sheets.

2. _____ The greenhouse air surrounding the treatment chamber was heated in winter by steam pipes. In summer, the greenhouse was cooled by pulling outside air through water-saturated pads on the south end of the building.

3. _____ Air enters and leaves the solar collector pipe through the air release vacuum breaker valves mounted at the highest point of the system.

4. _____ The JPL reactor was more heavily instrumented than the others for purposes of testing. In addition to inlet and outlet gas temperature measurements, 21 thermocouples were located in and on the converter.

5. _____ The quartz reactors tested for this work are fabricated by the Wm. A. Sales Company of Wheeling, Illinois. Both quartz reactors are configured as six-turn flat spirals, tube-in-tube, over the entire length.

6. _____ Liquid from the wall of the column was directed to the holding chamber and then was carried to the boiler via a liquid level controller which was specifically designed for this application.

Using Active and Passive Voice in Describing Materials

Both active and passive voice verb constructions are used in describing experimental materials. Your decision to use active or passive voice depends partly on whether the verb is *transitive* or *intransitive*. Only *transitive verbs* can be used in the passive voice. (Your dictionary will tell you if a given verb is transitive or intransitive.)

If the verb is transitive, follow these rules to determine which voice to use:

1. The *passive voice* is usually used when a human agent (the experimenter) is manipulating the materials.

HUMAN AGENT INVOLVED: Passive Voice

EXAMPLE A: The temperature inside the chamber *was increased* from 0° to 20°C. (The researcher increased the temperature.)

EXAMPLE B: Four thermocouples *were monitored hourly.* (A researcher monitored them.)

---

2. The *active voice* is usually used when no human is directly responsible for manipulating the materials—that is, when the materials operate "by themselves."

NO HUMAN AGENT INVOLVED: Active Voice

EXAMPLE C: A 200 hp generator *provided* power to the piezometers.

EXAMPLE D: Control gauges *monitored* air pressure inside the chamber.

In examples C and D, the use of the active voice indicates that the experimenters were not directly involved in the functioning of the equipment.

3. The passive voice may be used to describe an action involving a nonhuman agent, but a *phrase* must be included to indicate the agent.

NO HUMAN AGENT INVOLVED: Passive Voice

EXAMPLE E: Power was supplied *by 14 generators* with capacities ranging from 90 to 300 KW.

EXERCISE 6.7 Sentence Construction

Following are two lists, one of verbs and the other of nouns. Match each verb with an appropriate noun and write a sentence using these two words that might occur in a description of *materials*. Use either the *active* or *passive* voice, depending on (1) whether the verb is *transitive* or not; and (2) if transitive, whether you wish to indicate that a *human agent* was involved in the action.

NOUNS	VERBS
temperature	design
questionnaire	control
students	test
air pressure	select
generator	produce
solar collector	rise
sample	decrease
growth rate	measure
population	enter
water	consist of

EXERCISE 6.8 Identification

Read the section here describing the design of a solar hot water system. Refer to the accompanying diagram. Underline all examples of verbs in the active voice once. Underline passive voice verbs twice. Also, determine if the material described is *conventional* or *specially designed*.

HOW AN ACTIVE DUAL-TANK SOLAR HOT WATER SYSTEM WORKS

[1]Solar systems designed to heat water are now common in private homes in many parts of the country. [2]A typical domestic water heating system consists of three principal parts, which are: (A) roof mounted solar collectors, (B) a solar storage tank, and (C) an existing water heater. [3]Water is pumped through the south-facing collectors by a circulation pump (D). [4]As water passes through the collectors, it acquires heat and returns to the storage tank. [5]When hot water is needed, it is taken from the existing

water heater (C) and replaced by solar heated water. **6**An electronic control turns the pump on only during those hours when usable solar energy can be collected. **7**It also activates the drain-down valve (E) to drain the system when the collectors sense a freeze, or when the storage tank is completely charged with thermal energy.

    8The existing water heater serves as a back-up unit during long periods of cloudy weather, or when demand is unusually high. **9**Otherwise, its energy consumption is eliminated as long as the solar water temperature is higher than the existing water heater's thermostat setting.

_____ conventional equipment   _____ specially designed equipment

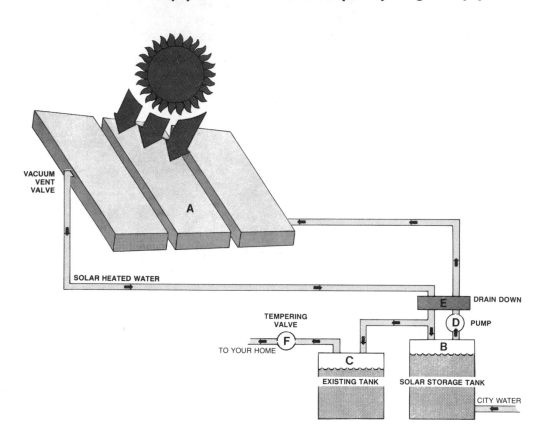

FIGURE 6.5   Solar water heating system.

EXERCISE 6.9　Fill-in

The description of the solar system is given again here. This time, without looking back at the original, fill in each blank with an appropriate *active or passive verb* or *auxiliary* in the correct tense. Refer to the figure if necessary.

1Solar systems designed to heat water _____ now common in private homes in many parts of the country. **2**A typical domestic water heating system _____ of three principal parts, which are: (A) roof-mounted solar collectors, (B) a solar storage tank, and (C) an existing water heater. **3**Water _____ through the south-facing collectors by a circulation pump. (D) **4**As water _____ through the collectors, it acquires heat and returns to the storage tank. **5**When hot water is needed, it _____ taken from the existing water heater (C) and replaced by solar heated water. **6**An electronic control turns the pump on only during those hours when usable solar energy can be _____. **7**It also activates the drain-down valve (E) to drain the system when the collectors _____ a freeze, or when the storage tank _____ completely charged with thermal energy.

　8The existing water heater _____ as a back-up unit during long periods of cloudy weather, or when demand is unusually high. **9**Otherwise, its energy consumption _____ eliminated as long as the solar temperature _____ higher than the existing water heater's thermostat setting.

EXERCISE 6.10　Reconstruction

The same materials description you have been practicing with is again given here, but this time the sentences are indicated only by lists of key words. Without referring back to the original, write out one sentence from each group, using *active* or *passive* constructions for the verbs as needed, in the correct tense. Add all necessary words and word endings so that each group forms a grammatical sentence. The key words are grouped and listed in the correct order.

1. solar systems
   now common
   private homes
   many parts
   country

2. typical
   solar hot water system
   three principal parts
     solar collectors
     solar storage tank
     existing water heater

3. as water
   circulate
   through collectors
   acquire heat
   return
   storage tank

4. when hot water
   need
   take
   existing water heater
   replace
   solar heated water

5. existing water heater
   serve
   back-up unit
   long periods
   cloudy weather
   or
   demand
   unusually high

EXERCISE 6.11   Library

From the photocopied materials description you obtained for Library Exercise 6.4, choose one paragraph and analyze all the sentences. Answer the following questions:

1. What *verb tense(s)* is used to describe the material?
2. What *voice* is used for each main verb (active or passive)?
3. Do the choices of tense and voice made by the author of your selection follow the conventions you have studied in this chapter?

INTEGRATION

EXERCISE 6.12   Guided Writing

The accompanying diagram shows two domestic hot water heaters run by electricity. The heater on the left is a *conventional* model commonly used in most homes. The heater on the right is an *experimental* model, modified with several features to save energy. Assume that you have conducted an experiment to test and compare the energy efficiency of the two models. Now write up the *materials* section of your report and briefly describe the modified heater in relation to the conventional design. Be sure to consider the following questions:

1. What kinds of information will you include, and how will you order them?
2. What verb tenses will you need to describe the materials?
3. What voice will you use for each verb?

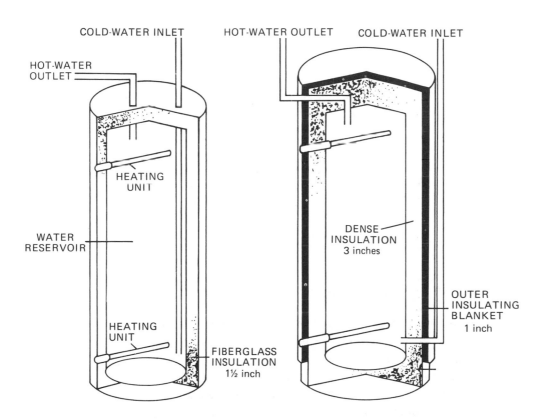

FIGURE 6.6   Conventional and experimental hot water heaters.

EXERCISE 6.13   Guided Writing

The following outline describes a questionnaire used in the study of job
satisfaction among construction workers that you wrote about in Chapter 5
(see Exercise 5.13.). Using the information contained in the outline, write a
description of the questionnaire as if you were the researcher, describing
materials in a report about this study. (The questionnaire was modified
from one used in previous studies.)

Materials

Questionnaire: Modified version of Michigan Organizational
Assessment Package

A.   Develop: Institute for Social Research, University of
Michigan

B.   Ask workers: indicate level of importance attached to 28
selected job outcomes (for example, salary, safety, benefits,
skills learned)

C.   Use 7-point scale (from 1, "Not Very Important," to 7,
"Extremely Important"

|----|----|----|----|----|----|----|
 1   2   3   4   5   6   7

D.   Ask workers: consider each question in context of present
job

EXERCISE 6.14   Writing Up Your Own Research

In previous chapters you have been conducting and writing up an original
research project of your own. You have already completed the introduction
and described the procedures you used (Chapters 2, 3, 4, and 5). Now
write about the *materials* that you used. Include a description of the sample
you used, the population it represents, and any equipment, apparatus, or
measurement tools you used. Finally, determine whether to integrate this
materials description with the procedural description you wrote previously.

Before you write, remember the following points:

1. Materials are described differently depending on whether they are *conventional* or *specially designed*.
2. When describing specially designed materials, the order of information follows a *three-part sequence*.
3. The description of principal parts may be arranged *functionally* or *spatially*.
4. *Verb tenses* are determined by the kind of materials being described.
5. *Verb voice* depends on the specific verbs you use and whether or not you are referring to a human agent.

CHECKLIST FOR CHAPTER 6

Describing Materials

INFORMATION

_____ Integrate the materials description with the procedural description.

_____ Briefly identify conventional materials.

_____ Use three-step order for describing specially designed materials.

_____ Choose spatial or functional arrangement when describing principal parts.

LANGUAGE

_____ Use past tense when describing the sample.

_____ Use present tense when describing the larger population.

_____ Use past tense when describing specially designed materials.

_____ Use present tense when describing conventional materials.

_____ Use active voice if the verb is intransitive and the action happens "by itself."

_____ Use passive voice if the verb is transitive and a human agent is involved in the action.

7

RESULTS

OVERVIEW

In this chapter we examine the third major section of the experimental research report, called **results**, in which you present the findings of your study and briefly comment on them. Some writers call this section "results and discussion," thus indicating more extensive comments on the findings of the study. However, in this chapter we follow the convention of including only brief comments focused on the statistical analysis, reserving the more general comments for a later section. Before you write this part of your report, check with your professor or editor to find out which organizational format you should follow.

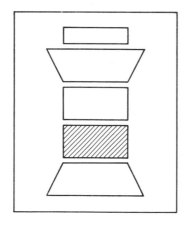

FIGURE 7.1   Results.

INFORMATION CONVENTIONS

The results section of the report presents the findings of the study in both *figures* and in written *text*. Figures (graphs, tables, and diagrams) present the complete findings in numerical terms, while the accompanying text helps the reader to focus on the most important aspects of the results and to interpret them. In this chapter we concentrate on the text, which usually consists of three main information elements. In the following selection from the field of foreign language education, these three elements have been identified for you.

FOREIGN LANGUAGE IN THE ELEMENTARY SCHOOL: A COMPARISON OF ACHIEVEMENT

location of results

[1]Figure 7.2 displays the mean percentile scores on the four subtests for non-immersion and immersion French students.

most important findings

[2]Students in the French immersion programs performed significantly better than their non-immersion peers on all four Modern Language Association tests by more than two to one in terms of scores attained on each of the subtests. [3]For example, in the listening subtest, immersion students scored at the 80th percentile, while non-immersion students scored at the 14th percentile. [4]Clearly, the

comments

findings indicate that the amount of exposure to a foreign language has a positive effect on student performance. [5]It appears that the intensity of immersion programs (an average of 75% of total instruction per week in French compared to approximately 10% for non-immersion) and use of the foreign language to study basic subjects results in substantial differences in performance in all four skill areas of the MLA test.

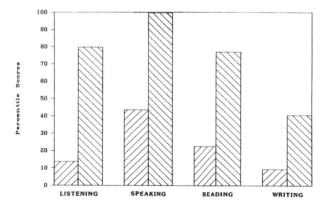

▨ NON-IMM ◺ IMM

FIGURE 7.2 Mean percentile scores by MLA subtest: French.

WHAT HAVE YOU OBSERVED?

1. Which sentences in the example present the actual results of the study?
2. How are the results of the study described in the first of these sentences?
3. Which findings from this study are described *numerically* in the text? Why do you think the authors chose to mention these particular data?

Ordering Your Information

The example just shown is typical of results sections in research reports in many fields. As you can see, this section consists of three basic elements of information.

RESULTS: Three Information Elements

ELEMENT 1: a statement that *locates the figure(s)* where the results can be found

ELEMENT 2: statements that *present the most important findings*

ELEMENT 3: statements that *comment* on the results

EXERCISE 7.1   Analysis

Read the following results section from a report in the field of child psychology. It describes the effects of a drug on boys who are overactive. Identify the sentences that correspond to the three elements listed in the preceding box.

DEXTROAMPHETAMINE: COGNITIVE AND BEHAVIORAL EFFECTS IN NORMAL PREPUBERTAL BOYS

Results

[1]The children left the testing center 3 hours after medication or placebo had been administered; parents were asked to keep a diary record of behavior during the afternoon and evening. [2]Behavioral and cognitive effects during the drug session are given in Figure 1 and Table 1.

[3]Behavioral ratings showed both immediate and delayed effects which differed from each other. [4]Amphetamine administration in comparison with placebo was associated with decreased motor activity combined with generally improved attentional performance (faster reaction time, superior memory and improved attention) and decreased galvanic skin response. [5]After drug administration, the children appeared unusually inactive, not simply less restless. [6]There was an increase in task-related descriptive speech and a decrease in speech not task-related, such as questions (Table 1). [7]These results are entirely consistent with those reported for hyperactive children on stimulant medication in previous studies (12).

1. Which sentence *locates the figure* where results can be found? _____

2. Which sentences present the *most important results?* _____

3. Which sentence *comments* on the results? _____

4. What is the function of the *first sentence* in the example? _____

_____

Alternate Short Form

Another ordering system for the results section is a *short form* of the ordering system we saw in the box on page 138. As you can see, in this alternative the three basic elements are reduced to two kinds of statements.

ALTERNATE SHORT FORM FOR PRESENTING RESULTS

ELEMENTS 1 AND 2 (combined): statements that present *the most important results* and that indicate in parentheses *the figure* where they can be found;

ELEMENT 3: statements that *comment* on the results.

EXAMPLE: Caffeine was somewhat more potent than theophylline in preventing leaf-eating (Figure 1). In contrast, caffeine has been reported elsewhere to be ten times weaker than theophylline as an adenosine antagonist (8).

EXERCISE 7.2   Identification

The following results section is from a paper in the field of civil engineering. It describes the types of organisms found in waste water treatment ponds. Identify which information elements are found in each sentence.

SOIL AND AQUATIC FUNGI IN A WASTE-STABILIZATION POND SYSTEM OF THE STATE OF MEXICO, MEXICO

Results

[1]A total of 53 samples were examined. [2]Direct microscopic examination of the samples showed 20 different fungal strains, which were isolated by culture and identified to the level of genus and/or species (Table 1). [3]These findings show that fungi can tolerate adverse environmental changes in the vegetative form. [4]Table 2 shows the results of the psychological tests applied to the isolates.

5None of the fungi strains was able to grow in culture media with 500 to 5000 mg L^{-1} of anionic surfactant. **6**An inhibitory effect on fungal growth and activity might be expected from the anionic surfactant level found in the ponds (Tomlinson and Williams, 1975).

Sentence 2: Elements _____
Sentence 3: Element _____
Sentence 4: Element _____
Sentence 5: Element _____
Sentence 6: Element _____

What is the function of Sentence 1 in this example? _____

NOTE: As we can see in the preceding example, an author may use both the three-step format and the shorter two-step alternative in the same results section.

Commenting on Results—Two Patterns

There are two possible ways to order your *comment statements* (Element 3). You may put a short comment (one or two sentences) after each significant result you mention, or you may leave your comments until all the results have been mentioned. The following box illustrates these two ways of ordering your comments.

TWO PATTERNS FOR ORDERING COMMENTS
(ELEMENT 3)

ALTERNATING PATTERN: $R_1 + C_1$; $R_2 + C_2$; $R_3 + C_3$

SEQUENTIAL PATTERN: $R_1 + R_2 + R_3 + C$

R = Results (Element 2); C = Comments (Element 3)

The *alternating pattern* is best if you have many individual results with specific comments about each result. The *sequential pattern* is used when there are several individual results to which one general comment applies. (Your professor or editor may ask you to put *all* comments in a separate section called "Discussion." See Chapter 8.)

EXERCISE 7.3   Analysis

Look at the two results sections that follow, both from the field of educational psychology. Decide whether the authors used the *alternating pattern* or the *sequential pattern* in commenting on their results.

A.   A COMPARISON OF HEMISPHERIC PREFERENCE
BETWEEN HIGH ABILITY AND LOW ABILITY
ELEMENTARY CHILDREN

Results

Results indicated that children in the high ability group responded as having significantly greater integrated hemispheric responses than did the low ability group [t(68) = 5.34, p < .01]. The low ability group responded with a significantly greater preference for right hemispheric responses [t(68) = 2.55, p < .01] than did the high ability group. In addition, the low ability group also displayed a significantly greater preference for the left hemispheric responses [t(68) = 4.87, p < .01] than did the high ability group (see Table 1).

The data from the two sub-categories measuring left or right hemispheric preferences suggest that the children who are displaying learning problems and who are not achieving up to the norm in school-related subjects are depending on one hemisphere and its mode of thought. Whether the dominance is on either the left or right cerebral hemisphere, the cognitive development of the low ability students is not adequate as evidenced by the placement of these children in special learning disability or educable mentally handicapped classes.

Pattern in example A: _____

B. FEARS OF SENEGALESE SECONDARY
SCHOOL STUDENTS

Results

The findings for the whole sample are summed by sex and by socioeconomic level in Table 1.

Family (7.1%). Students entered the following items: fear of my parents (2.9%), fear of my father (4.2%) (when he beats me, 1.5%; when he is furious 1.4%; when he chides me, 1.3%). That fathers should have such a high score results from the fact that Wolofs are an ethnic group reputed for the severity with which children are brought up (18). This severe education of the child seems to be mostly the responsibility of the father (20).

Imagination, supernatural phenomena (6.4%). Under this heading were entered sorcerers, evil genii, evil spirits, ghosts (4.1%), God (2.1%) and nightmares (.2%). A close comparison between the answers in the present questionnaire and those in Bariaud et al. (3) reveals that fear of nightmares (3.1%) is greater with the French sample than with ours. Conversely, fear of superstitions seems to be greater in Senegal. A tentative interpretation might be that in Senegal the supernatural seems to be part and parcel of everyday life, and nightmares are just one vehicle among several others expressing it. For the French students, on the contrary, the supernatural seems to boil down to irrational and naive superstitions that science and technology will soon eradicate. Nightmares, therefore, serve as the last socially acceptable outlet for all the fears and superstitions that have resisted scientific processing.

Animal (5.9%). This item remains important even for older students, which contradicts Bamber's (2) and Mauer's (13) findings. . . .

Pattern in example B: _____

Functions of Comments

The *comments* (Element 3) in results sections may serve a variety of different functions. Some of the most common functions are listed in the following box.

FUNCTIONS OF COMMENTS (ELEMENT 3)

Comments may: **1.** *generalize* from the results;
2. *explain* possible reasons for the results;
3. *compare* the results with results from other studies.

EXERCISE 7.4   Analysis

Each comment given here comes from a different research report. Determine the function of each according to the list in the preceding box.

a. _____ These data indicate that performance of *Rhizobium japonicum* strains is likely to be better under irrigated conditions.

b. _____ This difference in perceived time available for youth related activities is likely due to the additional amount of time spent on the job by divorced mothers.

c. _____ These findings accord with those from a larger study in which the same supplementation program increased birthweights by an average of 224 g in the months July to January (11).

d. _____ The reasons for this erratic pattern could be the age distribution of the children or the relatively small number of women in the sample with three or more children.

e. _____ Up to this point, these results are consistent with those of Chapman and Hutcheson (1982).

EXERCISE 7.5　Library

In your library locate the results section of an experimental research report in your field. Make a photocopy of the section and analyze it by answering the following questions.

1. Which *element of information* is represented by each sentence in your example?
2. Which *order* is used to present the information elements: the three-step format or the shorter two-step alternative?
3. Are *comment statements* (Element 3) included in the results section? If not, look at the report again to see if comments are presented in another section instead. If so, what is that section called?
4. If comments are written together with results, are they arranged according to the *alternating pattern* or the *sequential pattern*?
5. What *functions* do the comments serve?

LANGUAGE CONVENTIONS

The language conventions we look at in the results section of the report will help you to choose the appropriate *verb tense* or *modal auxiliary* for each element of information. We also examine some *special words and expressions* you can use to report different types of findings.

SEE WHAT YOU ALREADY KNOW　Pretest

Following is the results section from a report in the field of public health. The purpose of this study was to determine the effects of toxic chemicals on the birth weight of children born near a waste disposal area. Fill in each blank with any appropriate word.

INCIDENCE OF LOW BIRTH WEIGHT AMONG LOVE CANAL
RESIDENTS

Results

[1]The proportion of low birth weight infants among all live births was established for the entire study area, the swale area,

and the area abutting the canal. [2]Results _____ shown in Table 7.1 and Figure 7.3. [3]Among the 617 children born in the entire study area, 53 (8.6 percent) _____ low weight birth. [4]In the houses abutting the canal there _____ 124 live births with 8 (6.5 percent) low birth weight infants, and among the 174 live born infants in the swale area, 21 (12.1 percent) _____ low birth weights. [5]For the period of active dumping, the swale area's percentage of low weight births _____ higher than in upstate New York (z test, $P < 0.0001$) and the rest of the canal ($P < 0.012$) (see Figure 7.3). [6]Although it is clear that human exposure to a specific toxic agent _____ result in an adverse reproductive outcome, it is exceedingly difficult to define exposure in multi-chemical settings such as Love Canal. [7]Other variables, for which there are no objective data, _____ influence the frequency of these outcomes.

Table 7.1 Total Live Births and Children Born with Low Birth Weights

| | Number of births | | | | |
| | Swale | | Rest of canal | | |
History	Live	Low birth weight	Live	Low birth weight	P
All live births	174	21 (12.1)	443	32 (7.2)	0.027
Smoking					
Never smoked	70	7 (10.0)	174	7 (4.0)	0.035
Smoked	102	13 (12.7)	265	25 (9.4)	0.175
Household education					
< 12 years	41	6 (14.6)	105	3 (2.9)	0.004
12 to 15 years	124	14 (11.3)	285	24 (8.4)	0.179
≥ 16 years	7	1 (14.3)	44	0 (0.0)	

The P values are based on one-tailed z tests for two proportions. Numbers in parentheses are percentages.

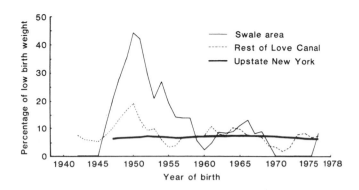

FIGURE 7.3   Five-year moving averages for percentages
of low birth rates.

Choosing Verb Tenses for Results

In using the three-step format to write your results section, you should observe the following verb tense conventions. In Element 1, use the *present tense* to locate your data in a figure.

ELEMENT 1: LOCATING THE FIGURE
Present Tense

EXAMPLE: Results of the t-tests *are presented* in Table 1.

EXAMPLE: Table 4 *summarizes* the test results on precontaminated insulators.

Notice in the examples in the box above that locational statements can be written in either the *active* or *passive voice*, but in both cases the *present tense* is used.

When you report your findings (Element 2), use the *past tense*.

ELEMENT 2: PRESENTING THE FINDINGS
Past Tense

EXAMPLE: As a group, divorced mothers *spent* over twice as much time in employment as married mothers (Figure 2).

EXAMPLE: The coefficient of correlation *was found* to be significant at the .001 level.

NOTE: In some fields such as engineering and economics, authors may present their findings in the present tense.

When *commenting* on the findings (Element 3), it is conventional to use the *present tense* or *modal auxiliaries*.

ELEMENT 3: COMMENTING ON THE RESULTS
Present Tense and Modal Auxiliaries

When the comment *compares* your results with the results of other studies, use the *present* tense.

EXAMPLE: This *is* consistent with earlier findings suggesting that personal characteristics *are* not related to attrition and teaching.

When the comment gives a *possible explanation* for the results, use a *modal auxiliary*.

EXAMPLE: These results $\begin{array}{c}can\\may\end{array}$ be explained by considering the voltage distribution on 230 kV insulators during freezing conditions.

When the comment *generalizes* from the results, use *may*.

EXAMPLE: Hyperactive children *may* be generally responsive to amphetamines.

In your Element 3 comments you may also use *tentative verbs* in the present tense instead of modal auxiliaries to generalize from results.

ELEMENT 3: COMMENTING ON THE RESULTS
Tentative Verbs

EXAMPLE: It $\begin{Bmatrix} appears \\ seems \\ is\ likely \end{Bmatrix}$ that hyperactive children are generally responsive to amphetamines.

EXAMPLE: These results *suggest* that children who display learning problems are depending on only one cerebral hemisphere.

EXERCISE 7.6   Analysis

Read the following excerpt from the results section of a report in the field of applied psychology. Underline the verb(s) in each sentence and complete the chart that follows.

AGE, EXPERIENCE AND PERFORMANCE ON SPEED AND SKILL JOBS IN AN APPLIED SETTING

Results

[1]Table 3 presents the data for workers holding skill jobs. [2]The overall piece rate was $6.03 per hour and the correlation between age and earnings was .26 ($p < .001$). [3]The older workers surpassed the younger ones and earned higher wages. [4]These results appear to reject the assumption that younger and older workers show equal productivity on skill jobs. [5]Forty accidents involving skill workers were reported for the calendar year (Table 3). [6]The reported cases were evenly split among workers younger than 45 and those age 45 and older. [7]In this case, the prediction of equivalent accident rates between age groups appears to be confirmed.

	VERB(S)	TENSE	FUNCTION
Sentence 1			
Sentence 2			
Sentence 3			
Sentence 4			
Sentence 5			
Sentence 6			
Sentence 7			

Element 2: Presenting Different Types of Findings

There are three different types of findings that you may need to report, depending on the kind of study you do. Specific words and expressions are used in writing about each type.

1. In some studies the findings involve a *comparison* among groups, often one or more experimental groups with a control group. In these cases Element 2 statements are often written using *comparative* or *superlative* expressions.

ELEMENT 2: COMPARISONS AMONG GROUPS

Group 1	Comparison	Group 2
The professional athletes	had *faster eye movements*	than our other subjects.
Quartz I reactors	had a *higher mass flow*	than Quartz II.

Superlative		Group 1
The *highest incidence* of Otitis Media		was found among Australian Indians.

---

2. In other studies the findings show the tendency of a variable to *fluctuate over time*. To report these kinds of results, use *expressions of variation* or special *verbs of variation* in your Element 2 statements.

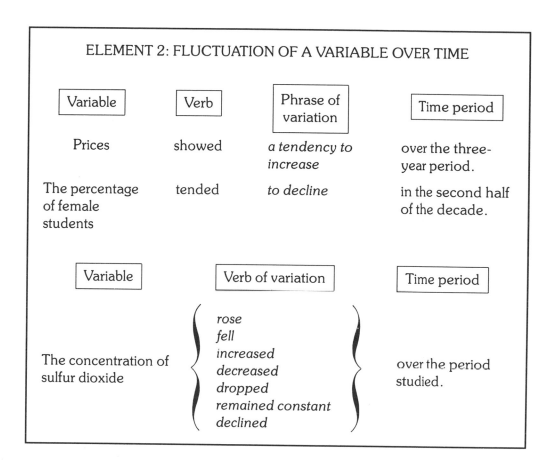

ELEMENT 2: FLUCTUATION OF A VARIABLE OVER TIME

Variable	Verb	Phrase of variation	Time period
Prices	showed	a tendency to increase	over the three-year period.
The percentage of female students	tended	to decline	in the second half of the decade.

Variable	Verb of variation	Time period
The concentration of sulfur dioxide	rose / fell / increased / decreased / dropped / remained constant / declined	over the period studied.

3. Findings of a third type show the relationship of one variable with another, or relationships among variables. When you report these kinds of results, it is common to use *verbs of correlation or association* in Element 2.

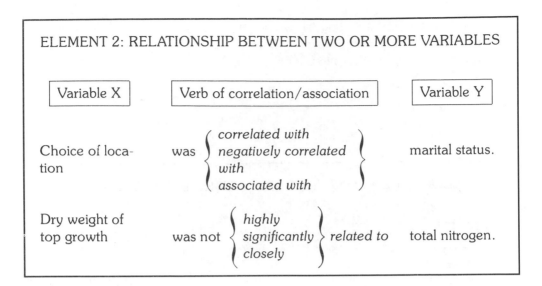

ELEMENT 2: RELATIONSHIP BETWEEN TWO OR MORE VARIABLES

Variable X	Verb of correlation/association	Variable Y
Choice of location	was { *correlated with* / *negatively correlated with* / *associated with* }	marital status.
Dry weight of top growth	was not { *highly* / *significantly* / *closely* } *related to*	total nitrogen.

EXERCISE 7.7 Interpretation

Look at each of the following figures. Decide whether the type of findings represented in each figure is comparison, variation, or correlation/association. Then write an Element 2 statement (or statements) indicating the most important results in each case.

A.   Table 7.2 Community Hearing Test Data

Age	Number Tested	Overall Percent	Number Passed	Number Failed	Percent Passed	Percent Failed
0–19	26	6.5%	26	0	100.0%	0.0%
20–29	89	22.1%	89	0	100.0%	0.0%
30–39	85	21.1%	79	6	92.9%	7.1%
40–49	64	15.9%	59	5	92.2%	7.8%
50–59	52	12.9%	33	19	63.5%	36.5%
60–69	62	15.4%	31	31	50.0%	50.0%
70–79	20	5.0%	7	13	35.0%	65.0%
80–89	5	1.2%	0	5	0.0%	100.0%
Total #	403	100%	324	79		

Type of finding in example A: _____

Possible Element 2 statement: _____

B. FIGURE 7.4 Enrollment in an intensive English program
(1973–1985).

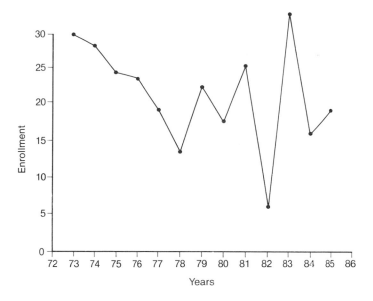

Years

Type of finding in example B: _____

Possible Element 2 statement: _____

C.   Table 7.3 Correlations between Age, Experience,
Hourly Rate and Absenteeism for Workers
in Skill and Speed Jobs

	Speed ($n = 212$)	Skill ($n = 455$)
Age × Experience	.69**	.61**
Age × Hourly Rate	.33**	.26**
Experience × Hourly Rate	.47**	.46**
Age × Absenteeism	−.24**	−.14*
Experience × Absenteeism	−.26**	−.25**

*$p < .01$. **$p < .001$.

Type of finding in example C: _____

Possible Element 2 statement: _____

EXERCISE 7.8   Identification

Read the following results selection from a study in psychology which was carried out to investigate the effects of space flight on astronauts. These results report the effect of weightlessness on the astronauts' eye movements during sleep. Underline the <u>verbs</u> in each sentence and identify their tenses. Be sure you understand why each tense is used.

EYE MOVEMENTS DURING SLEEP
IN WEIGHTLESSNESS

Observations. [1]During the first sleep period (night 0) in space, the number of eye movements increased dramatically compared with any of the pre- or post-flight nights, but it returned to normal by night 1 (Figure 7.5). [2]Similar fluctuations were seen in the percentage of rapid eye movement (REM) sleep as a function of total sleeping time. [3]On night 1, REM sleep increased to 50 percent, whereas it is normally between 20 and 25 percent of total sleeping time. [4]This abrupt increase is not pathological. [5]Instead, it reflects a temporary imbalance of the REM mechanisms which include other autonomic variables such as heart rate and blood pressure. [6]In pathological conditions, REM sleep decreases rather than increases.

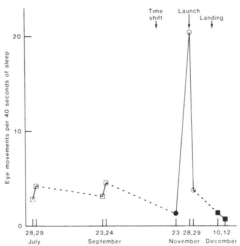

FIGURE 7.5   Number of eye movements per 40 seconds of sleep at various times.

EXERCISE 7.9 Fill-in

The results section from the study about space flight is given again here.
This time, without looking back at the original, fill in each blank space with
any appropriate *verb* or *auxiliary*.

EYE MOVEMENTS DURING SLEEP IN WEIGHTLESSNESS

Observations. [1]During the first sleep period (night 0) in space, the
number of eye movements _____ dramatically
compared with any of the pre- or post-flight nights, but it
_____ to normal by night 1 (Figure 7.5).
[2]Similar fluctuations _____ seen in the percentage of rapid
eye movement (REM) sleep as a function of total sleeping time.
[3]On night 1, REM sleep _____ to 50 percent,
whereas it _____ normally between 20 and 25 percent of
total sleeping time. [4]This abrupt increase _____ not pathological. [5]Instead, it _____ a temporary
imbalance of the REM mechanisms which include other autonomic
variables such as heart rate and blood pressure. [6]In pathological
conditions, REM sleep _____ rather than
increases.

EXERCISE 7.10 Reconstruction

The selection about space flight is given here again, but this time the sentences are indicated only by lists of key words. Without looking back at the
original, reconstruct one sentence from each list, using the correct *verb
tense* in each case. It is not necessary to change the order of the key
words; however, you will need to add some words and word endings to
make complete, grammatical sentences.

1. during
   first sleep period (night 0)
   space
   number of eye movements
   increase
   but
   return to normal
   night 1
   Figure 7.5

2. similar fluctuations
   see
   percentage of REM sleep
   function
   total sleeping time

3. on night 1
   REM sleep
   increase
   50 percent

4. abrupt increase
   not pathological

5. in pathological conditions
   REM sleep
   decrease
   rather than
   increase

EXERCISE 7.11   Library

Using the results example from the library that you photocopied for Library Exercise 7.5, analyze each sentence for the following features:

1. *Verb tense*
   a. What verb tense is used in each sentence?
   b. Explain why this particular tense is used.
   c. Do the tenses used in your library example follow the conventions you have learned here?

2. *Element 2 statements*
   a. What type of findings are presented — comparison among groups, fluctuation of a variable over time, or relationships among variables?
   b. What special verbs and phrases do the authors use to express these different types of findings?

INTEGRATION

EXERCISE 7.12   Guided Writing

Suppose that you have carried out a three-year study in the United States to determine people's attitudes towards education and specifically their willingness to finance public education projects through increased taxes. You have collected your data and have presented it in the figure below. Now write the text to accompany this graph. Include all the types of information that are conventionally included in a results section.

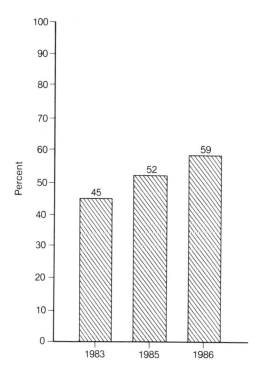

FIGURE 7.6   Percent of U.S. population favoring higher taxes for public education (1983–1986).

EXERCISE 7.13 Writing Up Your Own Research

In previous chapters you designed and carried out your own research project. You should now have the data necessary to begin writing up the results section of your report. Follow these steps.

1. Arrange your data in some convenient form for analysis, such as a large grid or table.
2. Apply any statistical procedures appropriate for your data and experimental design. If you do not have much background in inferential statistics, you might simply calculate totals, means, and percentages.
3. Construct a graphic (or graphics) in the form of tables or figures to illustrate your results.
4. Write a results text to accompany your graphic(s) following the conventions we have studied in this chapter. Consult the checklist which follows to remind yourself of these conventions.

CHECKLIST FOR CHAPTER 7

Describing Results

INFORMATION

_____ Include three elements of information in presenting results, in either long or short format.

_____ Write comments after each important finding, or put a general comment after the results.

_____ Write comments for various functions, depending on your findings.

LANGUAGE

_____ Use present tense to locate findings in a figure.

_____ Use past tense to indicate the most important findings.

_____ Use present tense or modal auxiliaries to comment on the findings.

_____ Use comparative and superlative expressions to report findings involving a comparison among groups.

_____ Use verbs and phrases of variation to describe variables that fluctuate over time.

_____ Use verbs of effect or association to report findings that involve relationships among variables.

DISCUSSION

OVERVIEW

In this chapter we look at the fourth section of the experimental research report. Usually titled **discussion**, it is the last major section of the report, followed by the list of references. In the discussion section you step back and take a broad look at your findings and your study as a whole. As in the introduction, researchers use the discussion section to examine their work in the larger context of their field.

Sometimes this section is called "conclusions" instead of "discussion." In either case, the writing conventions reflect some common features.

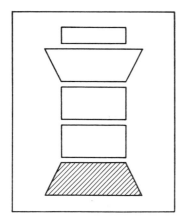

FIGURE 8.1   Discussion.

INFORMATION CONVENTIONS

As the shaded area representing discussion in Figure 8.1 suggests, this section moves the reader back from the *specific information* reported in the methods and the results sections to a more *general view* of how the findings should be interpreted.

Look at the following discussion section from a research report in the field of applied psychology. In this study the productivity of older and younger factory workers was compared. Notice the kinds of information that are included in this example.

AGE, EXPERIENCE, AND PERFORMANCE ON SPEED AND SKILL JOBS IN AN APPLIED SETTING

Discussion

original hypothesis

[1] The decremental theory of aging led us to infer that older workers in speed jobs would have poorer performance, greater absenteeism, and more accidents compared with other workers.

findings

[2] The findings, however, go against the theory. [3] The older workers generally earned more, were absent less, had fewer accidents, and had less turnover than younger workers. [4] One possible

explanation for findings

conclusion is that the requirements of the speed jobs in the light manufacturing industry under study do not make physical demands on the older workers to the limits of their reserve capacity. [5] The competence and experience of the older workers in these specific jobs may have compensated for their reduced stamina . . .

limitations

[6] This study has taken a step in the direction of defining the relationship between age, experience, and productivity in one particular industry. [7] It is possible of course that other industries with a different complex of speed jobs and skill jobs may produce entirely different results. [8] In addition, it is important to emphasize that methodological problems in the research design limit our interpretations.

need for further research

[9] The approach outlined in this study should be replicated in other manufacturing plants, as well as in other occupational areas in light, medium, and heavy industries in order to construct a typology of older worker performance in a variety of jobs.

WHAT HAVE YOU OBSERVED?

1. What did the authors of this study find out about their original hypothesis?
2. Why do you think the authors ordered the information in their discussion in the way shown here? What does the shape of the shaded area in Figure 8.1 indicate about this order?
3. What other kinds of information do you think the authors could have included in this section?

Ordering your Information

The information that you include in this section depends greatly on the findings of your study; however, the specific-to-general movement indicated by the shape of the shaded area in Figure 8.1 is a convention that most writers follow. The kinds of information that you can include in your discussion section are not fixed. However, the first elements are typically those that refer *most directly* to the study and its findings. They include:

FIRST INFORMATION ELEMENTS IN DISCUSSION:
Specific Reference to the Study

1. A reference to the *main purpose* or *hypothesis* of the study;

2. A review of the most important *findings*, whether or not they support the original hypothesis, and whether they agree with the findings of other researchers;

3. Possible *explanations* for or *speculations* about the findings;

4. *Limitations* of the study that restrict the extent to which the findings can be generalized.

As the discussion section continues, the writer moves the reader's attention away from the specific results of the study and begins to focus *more generally* on the importance that the study may have for other workers in the field.

LATER INFORMATION ELEMENTS IN DISCUSSION:
General Statements about the Study

5. *Implications* of the study (generalizations from the results);

6. *Recommendations* for future research and *practical applications*.

NOTE: The order of discussion elements shown here is not strictly followed by all authors. However, the progressive move from specific to more general information elements is conventional.

EXERCISE 8.1   Analysis

Read the following discussion section from a report in the field of management. The study was carried out to determine if management by objectives (MBO) practices would improve the quality and quantity of work and level of satisfaction of employees in a human services agency.

THE EFFECTS OF MBO ON PERFORMANCE AND SATISFACTION IN A PUBLIC SECTOR ORGANIZATION

Discussion

[1]The results of the satisfaction questionnaire were mixed. [2]Satisfaction with supervision significantly increased after implementation of the MBO program, and there was directional (but not significant) support that work satisfaction improved. [3]These results are consistent with previous research (Steers, 1976; Tosi et al., 1976). [4]Our findings thus lend support for the hypothesis that MBO leads to a satisfaction improvement, at least over the short term (Ivancevich, 1976). [5]Reliance on these measures must be tempered, however, because a control group was not available and only two measures were taken (before and after) in assessing changes in satisfaction.

[6]Because a high degree of variability was found in the data, it would be beneficial to replicate this study on larger and different populations. [7]It would also be interesting to measure satisfaction over several periods of time instead of for one pre- and one post-intervention. [8]The limitations in field experiments not withstanding, this study suggests that MBO may have a favorable impact on performance and satisfaction in public sector agencies. [9]Reinforcement of the MBO process and continuous reinforcement while using the system should aid in its acceptance and use.

Now identify the elements of information in the example that correspond to those listed in the boxes on page 162.

Sentences 1, 2, 3, and 4:	Information element _____
Sentence 5:	Information element _____
Sentences 6 and 7:	Information element _____
Sentence 8:	Information element _____
Sentence 9:	Information element _____

Researcher's Position towards the Findings

In the discussion section more than any other place in the report, researchers make explicit their own views on the study and its findings. The researcher may take a position with respect to the *explanations, implications, limitations,* or *applications* of the findings (Elements 3, 4, 5, and 6).

RESEARCHER'S POSITION ON INFORMATION IN THE DISCUSSION

Position	Information element
One possible explanation is	that speed jobs do not tax older workers to their limits. *(explanation)*
We can no longer assume	that it is satisfactory to seek explanations only in economic factors. *(implication)*
We acknowledge	that other industries may produce different results. *(restriction)*
Clearly,	this technique has promise as a tool in evaluation of forages. *(application)*

EXERCISE 8.2 Analysis

Each of the following statements comes from a different research report.
Determine the information element each sentence represents (see the first
two boxes earlier in this section) and indicate the element in the blank
space before each statement. Also underline the part of each sentence
that indicates the author's position towards the information.

1. _____ The present study offers clear
evidence that "hands-on experience" is not sufficient for the
productive learning of computer programming by novices.

2. _____ These findings lead us to believe
that more difficult materials should be used in order to give ESL
students additional practice in discerning implicit relationships
in English texts.

3. _____ What explains this larger than
expected gap between the two groups? It may be that dictating to a machine is faster than writing—at least for letters of
this type.

4. _____ We readily acknowledge that our
research is exploratory and that there are problems with the
statistical model.

5. _____ From our results, we suggest that
the optimal level of indentation for a computer program is 2–4
spaces.

6. _____ This finding is of considerable
importance since it suggests that the "resetting" of the metabolic machinery (25) is not confined to a single homeostatic
compartment.

EXERCISE 8.3 Arrangement

The discussion section from a research report in the field of sociology is given here, with the sentences in scrambled order. Rearrange and number the sentences in the order that you think the authors originally wrote them. Refer to the boxes on page 162, which show the typical sequence of information elements.

```
┌─────────────────────────────────────────┐
└─────────────────────────────────────────┘
```

SCHOLASTIC DISHONESTY AMONG COLLEGE UNDERGRADUATES

A. _____ We therefore recommend that colleges that wish to prevent cheating should not emphasize the social environment to the detriment of the intellectual environment.

B. _____ It seems clear that both theories are able to explain statistically significant amounts of variance in college cheating.

C. _____ The two perspectives examined were (1) culture conflict theory, and (2) internal social control theory.

D. _____ In the first case, we can expect that to the extent that a student has a high level of culture conflict orientation, he or she will have an increased probability of cheating.

E. _____ This research has attempted to assess two theories of deviant behavior in terms of their ability to account for cheating among a sample of college students (N = 650).

F. _____ Finally, since there was a surprising lack of consensus among the students in our sample on precisely which activities their faculty members were likely to see as forbidden, we further recommend that faculty members would do well to take time occasionally to clarify precisely what will be defined as "scholastic dishonesty" in their classes.

G. _____ On the other hand, to the extent that he has a high level of internal social control, his tendency to engage in cheating should be correspondingly reduced.

```
┌─────────────────────────────────────────┐
└─────────────────────────────────────────┘
```

EXERCISE 8.4 Library

In your library, find an experimental research report in your field (either a journal article, a thesis, or a dissertation). Locate the final section of the report and photocopy it. Then answer the following questions.

1. Look at the title of the last major section of the report. Is this section labeled "discussion"? If not, what is it called?
2. Identify each information element contained in the final section of your example. Use the boxes listing information elements for reference.
3. Do any of the sentences in the discussion indicate the *author's position* towards the information presented? If so, underline the phrases in which these positions are indicated.

LANGUAGE CONVENTIONS

In this part of the chapter we examine the sentence structure used in the discussion section to present elements of information and to give a point of view about that information. We also look at the verb forms that commonly occur in this section and at some of the special expressions authors use to indicate their positions towards the information they present.

SEE WHAT YOU ALREADY KNOW Pretest

Following is a portion of the discussion section from a report in the field of child psychology. The report compared the behaviors of overly competitive and less competitive children. Fill in each blank with any appropriate word.

[_____]

TYPE A BEHAVIORS BY CHILDREN, SOCIAL COMPARISON,
AND STANDARDS FOR SELF-EVALUATION

Discussion

[1]We initially _____ that Type A children would set higher standards than Type B children in evaluating their own performance. [2]These results support that hypothesis. [3]Type A children in this study _____ their own perform-

ance with that of a superior child even when they had been repeatedly told that their performance represented a "pretty good" score. **4**One _____ of this finding is that Type A children's awareness of high standards may trigger their attempts to achieve ever higher goals. **5**These findings _____ consistent with previous research (Pepitone, 1972), and they provide support for the hypothesis _____ ambiguous standards (or no standards) for evaluation of performance _____ be one factor that leads children to adopt high performance standards.

Complex Structure in Discussion Statements

To accommodate the information requirements of the discussion section, writers often use statements that are complex in grammatical structure—that is, that contain a main clause and a *noun clause*. Typically, the researcher's position is carried by the main clause while the information being reported is contained in the noun clause.

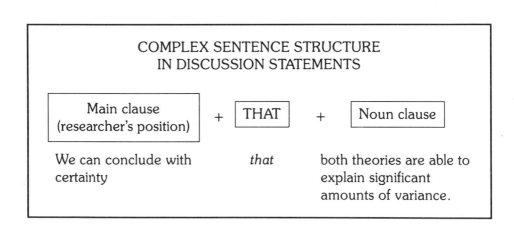

COMPLEX SENTENCE STRUCTURE
IN DISCUSSION STATEMENTS

Main clause (researcher's position) + THAT + Noun clause

We can conclude with certainty | *that* | both theories are able to explain significant amounts of variance.

EXERCISE 8.5 Analysis

Read the following discussion section from a report in social psychology whose purpose was to identify the attitudes and opinions that affect driving behavior. Then identify the sentences that contain a complex structure like the one shown in the preceding box.

INTERPERSONAL FACTORS IN DRIVING

[1]The results of the present study may be summarized by pointing out, firstly, that respondents regarded other people, and especially other drivers, as a major source of risk on the road. [2]This was largely attributed to qualities of the other driver such as carelessness, aggressiveness, discourtesy, selfishness, arrogance and the like. [3]Thus, the findings support the view that people think about safety on the road in terms other than objective features such as road conditions, state of vehicle repair, and so on. [4]Judgements about other drivers frequently involved interpretations about their personalities and temperaments, inferred from observable behavior. [5]A person might, for example, on noticing that a driver cut in sharply, conclude that he was dealing with an arrogant, ill-mannered, impatient young devil, and react accordingly, regardless of the facts of the situation. [6]This suggests that reactions to driving situations are not fully determined by the objective facts, but that they are influenced by subjective psychological factors, including drivers' assigning attitudes and values to each other.

[7]The present authors would argue that future research into driving and traffic behavior must use the insights of the full range of disciplines within the social sciences. [8]The study reported in the present paper has many shortcomings, but it does seem to demonstrate that a previously neglected approach to driving behavior— an approach based on concepts of social psychology—could lead to new important findings about the driving process.

Sentences with complex (noun clause) structures: _____

Verb Tenses Used in Discussion Statements

The verb tenses used in the discussion section depend on the type of information you want to present. Remember that the first information elements of the discussion refer specifically to the study and its findings. The verb tense most commonly used in referring to the purpose, the hypothesis, and the findings is the *simple past*.

VERB TENSES IN FIRST DISCUSSION ELEMENTS:
Simple Past Tense

Referring to the purpose

EXAMPLE: This research *attempted* to assess two theories of behavior.

Referring to the hypothesis

EXAMPLE: We originally *assumed* that physical decrements would be more apparent in speed jobs than in skill jobs.

Restating the findings

EXAMPLE: The principle of readability *was not followed* in the income tax booklet of any of the states studied except Virginia.

NOTE: In some fields the *present perfect* tense may be used in referring to the *purpose*.

In discussion statements that explain possible reasons for, or limitations to, the findings, the *past, present*, or *modal auxiliaries* may be used. The choice depends on whether the explanation for the specific findings is *restricted* to your study (past) or whether it refers to *a general condition* (present). Modal auxiliaries may also be used to emphasize the speculative nature of these statements.

```
┌─────────────────────────────────────────────────────────────────┐
│                                                                   │
│         VERB TENSES IN FIRST DISCUSSION ELEMENTS:                 │
│            Past, Present, and Modal Auxiliaries                   │
│                                                                   │
│   ┌──────────────────────────────┐                               │
│   │ Explaining the findings      │                               │
│   └──────────────────────────────┘                               │
│                                                                   │
│   EXAMPLE: It is possible that microbial activity *caused* some im-│
│            mobilization of labial soil phosphorous. *(restricted to│
│            study)*                                                │
│                                                                   │
│   EXAMPLE: It is possible that microbial activity *causes* some immo-│
│            bilization of labial soil phosphorous. *(general condi-*│
│            *tion)*                                                │
│                                                                   │
│   ┌──────────────────────────────┐                               │
│   │ Limiting the findings        │                               │
│   └──────────────────────────────┘                               │
│                                                                   │
│   EXAMPLE: Our sample *was* very small.                          │
│                                                                   │
│   EXAMPLE: Other industries *may produce* different results.     │
│                                                                   │
└─────────────────────────────────────────────────────────────────┘
```

When comparing your findings to those of other researchers, use the *present tense*.

```
┌─────────────────────────────────────────────────────────────────┐
│                                                                   │
│         VERB TENSES IN FIRST DISCUSSION ELEMENTS:                 │
│                      Present Tense                                │
│                                                                   │
│   ┌──────────────────────────────┐                               │
│   │ Comparing findings           │                               │
│   └──────────────────────────────┘                               │
│                                                                   │
│   EXAMPLE: These results *are* in substantial agreement with those│
│            of Bates (2).                                          │
│                                                                   │
└─────────────────────────────────────────────────────────────────┘
```

As you move from the specific considerations of your study to broader, more general statements about the importance of the study as a whole, use *simple present tense* and *modal auxiliaries/tentative verbs*.

```
┌─────────────────────────────────────────────────────────────┐
│              VERB TENSES IN LATER ELEMENTS:                  │
│           Present and Modal Auxiliaries/Tentative Verbs      │
│                                                             │
│                                                             │
│   ┌──────────────┐                                          │
│   │ Implications │                                          │
│   └──────────────┘                                          │
│                                                             │
│   EXAMPLE: It appears that squatter housing markets behave as│
│            economically rational entities.                   │
│                                                             │
│                                                             │
│   ┌────────────────────────────────┐                        │
│   │ Recommendations and applications │                      │
│   └────────────────────────────────┘                        │
│                                                             │
│   EXAMPLE: The approach outlined in this study should be repli-│
│            cated in other manufacturing plants.              │
│                                                             │
│   EXAMPLE: We recommend that the approach outlined in this   │
│            study be replicated in other manufacturing plants.│
│                                                             │
└─────────────────────────────────────────────────────────────┘
```

EXERCISE 8.6 Analysis

Read the following excerpt from a discussion section in the field of computer science. The study tested the effect of two styles of indentation and four levels of indentation on the ability of novice and expert subjects to understand a computer program.

PROGRAM INDENTATION AND COMPREHENSIBILITY

. . . [1]The results indicate that the level of indentation has a significant effect on program comprehension and that deeper indentation could become more of a hindrance than an aid. [2]The level of indentation that seems to produce optimal results in comprehension is between 2 and 4 spaces; as the number of spaces increases, the comprehension level decreases. [3]The blocked and nonblocked styles of the program yielded no significant differences between the experts and the novices. [4]We are not sure how to explain these results because we expected a significant difference in comprehension between the two styles. **5**It is possible that comprehension scores for a longer and more complex program would show a greater difference.

6We believe future experiments should employ the measure of program comprehension and recommend that 9 indentation levels (0 to 8 spaces) be studied. **7**Moreover, the blocking style should be consistent throughout a program so that users can easily find the statement or statement segment they are trying to locate.

Now underline the verbs and modal auxiliaries you found in the preceding example and complete the following chart by writing down (1) the verb(s); (2) the tense of the verb(s); and (3) the information element represented by each sentence. (Because this is only a portion of a discussion section, let the verb tense guide you in identifying the information element.)

	VERBS	TENSE	INFORMATION ELEMENT
Sentence 1			
Sentence 2			
Sentence 3			
Sentence 4			
Sentence 5			
Sentence 6			
Sentence 7			

Expressions Indicating the Researcher's Position

The main clause of a complex sentence in the discussion section often contains special expressions that indicate the researcher's own point of view, or position, towards the information contained in the noun clauses. At the beginning of the discussion section, certain expressions make it clear that you are reconsidering *the hypothesis* of your study.

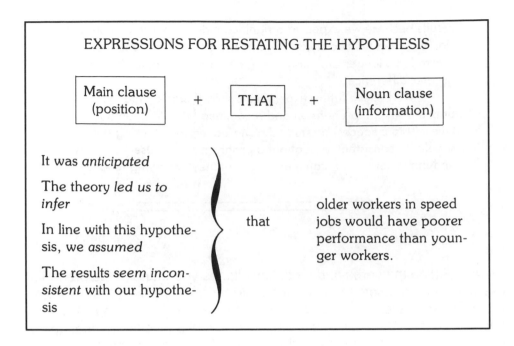

EXPRESSIONS FOR RESTATING THE HYPOTHESIS

| Main clause (position) | + | THAT | + | Noun clause (information) |

It was *anticipated*

The theory *led us to infer*

In line with this hypothesis, *we assumed*

The results *seem inconsistent* with our hypothesis

} that older workers in speed jobs would have poorer performance than younger workers.

Other expressions are typically used when you need to *explain* your findings.

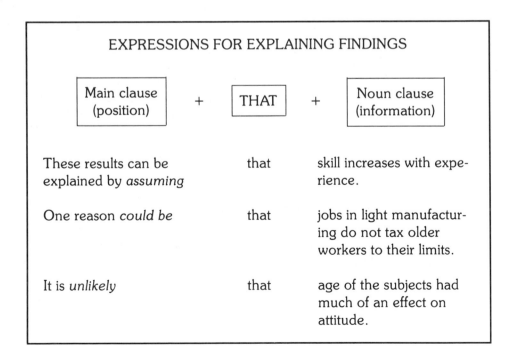

EXPRESSIONS FOR EXPLAINING FINDINGS

| Main clause (position) | + | THAT | + | Noun clause (information) |

These results can be explained by *assuming* — that — skill increases with experience.

One reason *could be* — that — jobs in light manufacturing do not tax older workers to their limits.

It is *unlikely* — that — age of the subjects had much of an *effect* on attitude.

Still other expressions are used when you wish to suggest the *implications* of your findings.

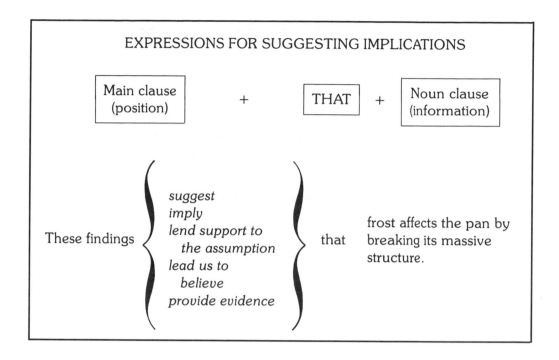

EXPRESSIONS FOR SUGGESTING IMPLICATIONS

| Main clause (position) | + | THAT | + | Noun clause (information) |

These findings { suggest / imply / lend support to the assumption / lead us to believe / provide evidence } that frost affects the pan by breaking its massive structure.

EXERCISE 8.7 Sentence Construction

Following are a number of discussion statements from various studies. The information element contained in each is indicated in parentheses. Rewrite each statement as a complex sentence with a *noun clause* by adding an appropriate expression at the beginning of each element.

1. (implication) An increase in chlorine emission is accompanied by a corresponding increase in noise, so that the detection limit remains constant.

2. (explain results) The addition of water to the powder diet released certain flavors and odors that enhanced palatability.

3. (refer to hypothesis) MBO would lead to an improvement in the quality of performance.

_____

4. (recommendation) More forethought and planning are required before training received in developed countries can be optimally used in less developed countries.

_____

5. (explain findings) The 14-day periods during which steers were fed diets containing monensin may not have been long enough for the full effect of the antibiotic to be expressed.

_____

6. (explain findings, negative) Significant details, invisible to the naked eye, and visible only to 3-D processing, could have been added to the Shroud of Turin.

_____

EXERCISE 8.8   Identification

Read the following discussion section from a study in the field of economics. The study investigated the monetary value of illegal, informal housing in the urban areas of developing countries. Underline the <u>verbs</u> and <u>modal auxiliaries</u> in each sentence and identify the tenses. Explain why each tense is used by indicating the information element that each statement represents.

THE VALUE OF SQUATTER DWELLINGS IN DEVELOPING COUNTRIES

Discussion

1This study has used data from the Philippines to determine whether a squatter-owner's valuation of his own house would compare with that of an independent appraiser. **2**The results show that discrepancies in the estimates were quite large for individual properties. [3]However, these discrepancies were largely offset when the averages for reasonably sized samples were compared. [4]This confirms earlier findings by Kain and Quigley (1972) for conventional housing in the United States. [5]Overall, it appears that squatter housing markets behave as economically rational entities similar to conventional markets. [6]They should be accounted for in any analysis regarding housing markets in developing countries.

EXERCISE 8.9   Fill-in

The discussion section from the report about squatter housing is given again here. This time, without looking back at the original, fill in each blank space with any appropriate word.

Discussion

[1]This study _____ data from the Philippines to determine whether a squatter-owner's valuation of his own house _____ compare with that of an independent appraiser. [2]The results show _____ discrepancies in the estimates were quite large for individual properties. [3]However, these discrepancies were largely offset when the averages for reasonably sized samples were compared. [4]This _____ earlier findings by Kain and Quigley (1972) for conventional housing in the United States. [5]Overall, it _____ that squatter housing markets behave as economically rational entities similar to conventional markets. [6]They _____ be accounted for in any analysis regarding housing markets in developing countries.

EXERCISE 8.10 Reconstruction

The selection about squatter housing is given here once again, but this time the sentences are indicated only by lists of key words. Without looking back at the original, reconstruct one sentence from each list, using the correct verb tense and/or modal auxiliary in each case. It is not necessary to change the order of the key words; however, you will need to add some words and word endings to make complete, grammatical sentences.

1. this study
   data from the Philippines
   determine whether
   squatter-owner's valuation
   own house
   compare
   independent appraiser

2. results show
   discrepancies in estimates
   quite large

3. however, these
     discrepancies
   largely offset
   when averages
   reasonably sized samples
   compared

4. confirm
   earlier findings
   Kain and Quigley (1972)
   conventional housing
   United States

5. overall
   appear
   squatter housing markets
   behave
   economically rational
     entities
   similar to conventional
     markets

6. they
   be account for
   any analysis
   housing markets
   developing countries

LIBRARY EXERCISE 8.11

Select one paragraph from the discussion example that you found for Library Exercise 8.4 and analyze each sentence, answering the following questions:

1. What verb tense or modal auxiliary is used in each sentence?
2. Can you explain why each tense or auxiliary is used?

3. Do the verb tenses or auxiliaries used in your example agree with the conventions you have learned here? What differences did you find?
4. What special expressions did the researcher(s) use to indicate a position towards the information in the discussion?

INTEGRATION

EXERCISE 8.12　Guided Writing: Discussion

The following research report describes a study from the field of extension and home economics. It deals with the differences in perceptions that married and divorced mothers have about the way they spend their time during a typical work day. Read the entire report carefully. Then write a discussion section for the report. Keep in mind the kinds of information that can be included in a discussion section:

1. a reference to the *hypotheses or assumptions* that underlie the study;
2. a review of the most important *findings* of the study, their relation to the initial hypotheses, and possible *explanations* for the findings;
3. a *comparison* with the results of other studies;
4. the *limitations* of the study;
5. *implications* for practical application and *suggestions* for further research.

HOW IS THE TIME SPENT? A LOOK AT SOME STEREOTYPES OF
ONE- AND TWO-PARENT FAMILIES

Time is recognized as one of the most basic resources for families, but it is considered in short supply by many people. Individual perceptions of the adequacy of time to conduct daily affairs potentially affects management of time resources. How time is allocated and per-ceptions about the adequacy of time resources have implications for programming needs of all families, but especially for one-parent families.

The increase in the number of one-parent families in the past decade has been dramatic. Today, over 20% of families with children are maintained by a separated, divorced, widowed, or never-married parent(1). Among these families, 9 of 10 are maintained by mothers. One-fifth of children under 18 years of age presently live in a one-parent family, an increase of well over 50% in the past 10 years(2).

These changes in family structure have spurred concern about everyday life experiences in families maintained by one parent. Information about dysfunctional aspects of life in one-parent families is readily available(3), but there is little reliable information about day-to-day activities in these families. As Extension continues to address problems of families in achieving a quality of life, more information is needed about families in alternative lifestyles. One-parent families, particularly, are cited as a high priority audience for home economics programs (4).

To better understand everyday events and perception of the adequacy of their time resources, our 1981 study compared mothers in one-parent and two-parent families. The data from this study conducted in Oklahoma by the OSU Family Studies Center refute some stereotypes about differences between one-parent and two-parent families and provide the basis for programming recommendations.

Methodology

In our study, we interviewed divorced and married mothers in families identified through churches and social organizations. Each family had two children; the younger child was in elementary school, and the age of the older child ranged through high school. We conducted each interview in the family's home in the spring during the school year.

The mothers were predominately white, Protestant, and had attended college; most were 35 to 40 years of age. Twenty of the 30 married mothers and 27 of the 29 divorced mothers interviewed were employed, with administrative and professional occupations prevailing. Educational attainment and occupational status were higher than in the general population.

We asked mothers to respond to a set of statements about their perceived adequacy of resources, including time for personal and family roles. We also asked the mothers to recall how time was used in the previous 24-hour period, which was always a weekday, to provide data for comparison of time use in the two family types.

Findings

Results of t-tests of the mothers' responses on adequacy of time for various activities are presented in Table 8.1. Divorced mothers perceived their time to help children participate in organized youth activities and to do housework to be less adequate than married mothers. On other time demands, divorced and married mothers didn't differ in their perceptions of the adequacy of time.

These results deal with *perceived* time and provide an indication of time pressures divorced mothers face in regard to housework and children's activities. What about *actual* time use by mothers in the two family structures? Results of t-tests for difference in time use are in Table 8.2.

As a group, divorced mothers spent over twice as much time in employment as married mothers. Married mothers who were employed were more likely to hold part-time jobs compared to employed divorced mothers whose jobs tended to be full-time. Obviously, when a large amount of time is spent in one activity, time spent in some other activities must be reduced. Divorced mothers in our study spent only half as much time in housework as married mothers. They did less food preparation, clothing care and construction, and shopping compared to married mothers. Even though less time probably is needed to do housework for three people instead of four, we believe the wide difference in time spent by the two groups points to differences in lifestyles of the families.

The divorced mothers in our study averaged about two-thirds as much time in leisure pursuits as married mothers. The larger proportion of employed mothers in the divorced group probably explains this difference.

Contrary to popular myth that children in one-parent families receive less care from parents, divorced mothers in our study didn't spend a significantly different amount of time in family member care to married mothers. However, the way that time was spent did differ. Of the time divorced mothers spent in care of family members, one-third was used for transportation, while the married mothers used nearly half their family member care time for transportation.

The two groups of mothers didn't differ significantly in time spent in personal maintenance, which included sleeping, eating, and personal hygiene. Nor did they differ in time spent in other activities, which included unpaid work, school, organization attendance, and time for which no accounting was given.

Table 8.1 Mothers' Perceived Adequacy of Time

Statement	Mean response*	
	Divorced mothers	Married mothers
I have enough time for myself.	3.4	3.6
I have enough time for the activities that I want to do.	3.8	3.6
I have enough time to spend with my spouse (or a friend of the opposite sex).	4.0	4.1
I have enough time to spend with my children.	4.5	5.0
I have enough time to help my children participate in organized youth activities.	4.6**	6.2**
I have enough time for housework.	3.7**	4.5**

  * Scale: 1 = strongly disagree, 7 = strongly agree.
** Indicates significant difference at the .05 level.

Table 8.2 Mothers' Actual Time Use

Activity	Mean minutes on record day	
	Divorced mothers	Married mothers
Employment	424*	179*
Housework	136*	265*
Leisure	157*	227*
Family member care	76	94
Personal maintenance	571	597
Other activities	76	78

*Indicates significant difference at the .05 level.

EXERCISE 8.13 Writing Up Your Own Research

Following the model we have presented in this chapter, write the discussion section for your own research project. Use the Checklist for Chapter 8 to help you remember the information and language conventions that typify this part of the experimental research report. Before you begin to write the discussion, think about the following questions:

1. What assumptions or hypotheses did you have about your topic before you started your research?
2. Were your hypotheses confirmed?
3. What were your most important results?
4. Why do you think you obtained those particular results?
5. Were there any problems with the methodology of your study that may limit the generalizability of the results?
6. What important implications do your results have?
7. What is the next logical question for further research to pursue in investigating your topic?

CHECKLIST FOR CHAPTER 8

Discussion

INFORMATION

_____ Include various elements of information, depending on the problems encountered, results obtained, possible applications, and further research needed.

_____ Move from specific results to general implications.

LANGUAGE

_____ Use complex structures including noun clauses to express your position towards the findings.

_____ Use past tense to refer to the original hypothesis and to review your results.

_____ Use the simple present, simple past, or modal auxiliaries when explaining and limiting your results.

_____ Use the simple present tense to compare your findings with those of others.

_____ Use the simple present and modal auxiliaries or tentative verbs to make implications or recommendations or to suggest applications.

_____ Use special expressions to indicate your position towards any of the information elements included.

ABSTRACT

OVERVIEW

The last major section of the experimental research report we look at is the **abstract**. As you know, the abstract is actually the *first* section of a report, coming after the title and before the introduction. The abstract provides the reader with a brief preview of your study based on information from the other sections of the report. We have reserved our examination of the abstract for the last chapter because it is often the last part of the report to be written.

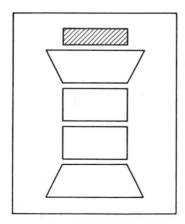

FIGURE 9.1   Abstract.

INFORMATION CONVENTIONS

Many readers depend on the abstract to give them enough information about the study to decide if they will read the entire report or not.

Read the following sample abstract from the field of computer science. It reports on a test of a voice recognition device designed to take dictation. Notice the kinds of information included and the order in which the information is presented.

COMPOSING LETTERS WITH A
SIMULATED LISTENING TYPEWRITER

background

purpose

method

results

conclusion

Abstract. **1**With a listening typewriter, what an author says would be automatically recognized and displayed in front of him or her. **2**However, speech recognition is not yet advanced enough to provide people with a reliable listening typewriter. **3**An aim of our experiments was to determine if an imperfect listening typewriter would be useful for composing letters. **4**Participants dictated letters, either in isolated words or in consecutive word speech. **5**They did this with simulations of listening typewriters that recognized either a limited vocabulary or an unlimited vocabulary. **6**Results indicated that some versions, even upon first using them, were at least as good as traditional methods of handwriting and dictating. **7**Isolated word speech with large vocabularies may provide the basis for a useful listening typewriter.

WHAT HAVE YOU OBSERVED?

1. What was the principal activity of this research project?
2. Why are the five information elements in the preceding abstract ordered in this particular way?
3. Which sentences could be eliminated from this abstract without losing critical information about the study?

Ordering Your Information

Abstracts from almost all fields of study are written in a very similar way. The types of information included and their order are very conventional. The box that follows shows the typical information format of an abstract.

```
┌─────────────────────────────────────────────────────┐
│          ORDER OF TYPICAL ELEMENTS INCLUDED           │
│                   IN AN ABSTRACT                      │
│                                                       │
│  B = some background information                      │
│  P = the principal activity (or purpose) of the study and its │
│        scope                                          │
│  M = some information about the methodology used in the │
│        study                                          │
│  R = the most important results of the study          │
│  C = a statement of conclusion or recommendation      │
└─────────────────────────────────────────────────────┘
```

NOTE: In some publications this section is titled "summary." Check with your editor or professor to determine the appropriate title for you to use.

EXERCISE 9.1   Analysis

Read the following abstract carefully. It is taken from the child psychology study that we saw in Chapter 8. Identify the sentences in the abstract that correspond to the elements *B, P, M, R*, and *C* in the preceding box.

TYPE A BEHAVIORS BY CHILDREN, SOCIAL COMPARISON, AND STANDARDS FOR SELF-EVALUATION

Abstract. [1]Type A behavior, an established risk factor for coronary heart disease, is characterized by extremes of competitive achievement striving, impatience, hostility, and aggression. [2]As part of an effort to understand the origins of this behavior pattern, the present study assessed the impact of performance standards on the social behavior of Type A and Type B children. [3]Children performed a five-trial task. [4]Half were given an explicit standard with which to compare their own performance; half were given no standard. [5]After 5 trials, all subjects were informed that their total score represented the middle score of the whole group and were asked to select one score for further comparison. [6]Results showed no significant differences among groups on the frequency of comparison. [7]In contrast, the results did show that regardless of the presence or absence of an explicit standard, Type A children chose to evaluate their performance against the top score, whereas Type B children chose to do so only in the absence of an explicit standard. [8]The implications of these results for understanding the childhood antecedents of Type A behavior are discussed.

B = Sentence(s) _____

P = Sentence(s) _____

M = Sentence(s) _____

R = Sentence(s) _____

C = Sentence(s) _____

Reducing the Abstract

Abstracts are usually written to be as brief and concise as possible. For journal articles the editor often establishes a word limit for the abstract that authors cannot exceed. In order to shorten an abstract to satisfy such limitations, you can eliminate or combine much of the information shown in the previous box.

The reduced abstract typically focuses on only two or three elements, with the emphasis placed on the *results* of the study. Information concerning the purpose and method is presented first (background information is not included). Then the most important results are summarized. Finally, conclusions and recommendations may be included in one or two sentences.

ORDER OF INFORMATION ELEMENTS
IN REDUCED ABSTRACTS

P + M = purpose and method of the study
R = results
C = conclusions and recommendations*

*optional

EXERCISE 9.2   Analysis

Read the following reduced abstract from a report in the field of business and economics dealing with the reading difficulty of tax information booklets. Identify the kinds of information that are included and then answer the four questions that follow.

THE READABILITY OF INDIVIDUAL INCOME TAX INSTRUCTION BOOKLETS IN SOUTH CAROLINA AND OTHER SOUTHEASTERN STATES

Abstract. [1]To determine the understandability of individual income tax booklets, a Reading Ease score was calculated for the 1977 Federal income tax return form 1040 and tax forms of nine southeastern states. [2]The instruction booklets of all states except Virginia were found to be at a reading level higher than the median educational level of the average citizen-taxpayer in those states. [3]The South Carolina booklet was three grade levels above the median education level for the state. [4]The Federal instruction booklet was easiest to read, falling four grade levels below the median education level of U.S. citizens. [5]If an equitable state income tax system is to be maintained, actions must be taken to reduce the disparity between median education levels and the readability of state income tax instruction booklets.

---

1. Which elements are included in sentence 1?
2. Which element is represented by the most number of sentences?
3. Which element is represented by the final sentence?
4. Which element has been eliminated?

EXERCISE 9.3   Reconstruction

Following is the abstract from a report in the field of computer programming. Read the abstract and analyze each sentence for the type of information it contains. Then write out a *reduced* version, combining method and purpose into one or two sentences and eliminating any nonessential elements.

PROGRAM INDENTATION AND COMPREHENSIBILITY

Abstract. [1]The consensus in the programming community is that indentation aids program comprehension, although many studies do not back this up. [2]We tested program comprehension on a Pascal program. [3]Two styles of indentation were used—blocked and nonblocked—in addition to four possible levels of indentation (0, 2, 4, 6 spaces). [4]Both experienced and novice subjects were used. [5]Although the blocking style made no difference, the level of indentation had a significant effect on program comprehension. [6]2–4 spaces had the highest mean score for program comprehension. [7]We recommend that a moderate level of indentation be used to increase program comprehension and user satisfaction.

EXERCISE 9.4 Arrangement

Each of the following sentences is taken from the abstract to a report in the field of economics. The sentences are not in their correct order. Indicate the probable order used by the author in writing the abstract.

THE DECENTRALIZATION OF AMERICAN ECONOMIC LIFE: AN INCOME EVALUATION

A. _____ This investigation provides a national analysis of these growth patterns by examining the behavior of three variables: change in per capita income, population deconcentration, and growth in economic productivity.

B. _____ The results suggest that the presence or absence of unique sets of industry factors can be used to explain growth variation in both the center and the periphery of the industrialized region.

C. _____ National economic and demographic growth patterns in the United States during the decade of the seventies show marked departures from what had occurred in previous times.

D. _____ Results of the analysis showed that a process of decentralization occurred, best described by center-periphery concepts.

EXERCISE 9.5 Library

In the library, find an experimental research report in your field (either a journal article, a thesis, or a dissertation). Make a photocopy of the first page and answer the following questions:

1. Does the report contain a brief preview section located before the Introduction? (If there is no preview, find another example.) Is this preview section titled "abstract"? If not, how is it titled?
2. Look at the abstract of the report and identify each sentence using the letters B, P, M, R, and C to indicate the kinds of information presented. Are all five elements included? If not, how has the abstract been reduced?
3. Does the abstract in your example contain more than 150 words? If it does, how could it be reduced to meet this limit?

LANGUAGE CONVENTIONS

The language features of the abstract correspond to those we have already seen in the four major portions of the experimental research report. Here we briefly review the conventions that govern the use of verb tenses, tentative verbs, and modal auxiliaries.

SEE WHAT YOU ALREADY KNOW   Pretest

An abstract from a report in the field of agronomy is given here. Fill in each blank space with any appropriate word.

ROW SPACING, PLANT POPULATION AND WATER MANAGEMENT EFFECTS ON CORN IN THE ATLANTIC COASTAL PLAIN

Abstract. [1]Lack of water because of erratic rainfall frequently _____ corn production in the Atlantic Coastal Plain. [2]Traditionally, wide (96 cm) row spacing and low plant population have been used to prevent water stress, but recently landowners have begun to invest in irrigation systems. [3]We _____ plant population treatments averaging 7.0 and 10.1 plants m^{-2} in single and twin rows on a Norfolk loamy sand during 1980, 1981, and 1982. [4]Three water treatment and two fertilization programs _____ also evaluated in a four-factor split-plot design. [5]Water management and plant population interacted significantly. [6]Planting in twin rows _____ grain production an average of 0.64 Mg ha^{-1} (10 bu/A), but planting more than 7.1 plants m^{-2} significantly increased grain yield only in 1980. [7]Irrigation _____ grain yield by 150, 161, and 8% in 1980, 1981, and 1982, respectively. [8]Increasing total N, P, and K fertilizer applications beyond 200, 30, and 167 kg ha^{-1}, respectively, _____ not significantly influence grain yield or yield components. [9]Yield advantages of narrow rows _____ be obtained on Coastal Plain soils by using a twin-row planting configuration. [10]Irrigation _____ be scheduled using either tensiometers or a computerized water balance without significantly changing corn grain yield, nutrient accumulation, or yield components.

Verb Tenses in the Abstract

The verb tenses used in writing sentences in the abstract are directly related to those you used in the corresponding sections earlier in your report. For example, background (*B*) sentences in the abstract are similar to background sentences in Stage I of the Introduction: They both are written in the *present tense*.

ABSTRACT: Verb Tenses

B   Background information (present tense)

EXAMPLE: One of the basic principles of communication *is* that the message should be understood by the intended audience.

P   Principal activity (past tense/present perfect tense)

EXAMPLE: In this study the readability of tax booklets from nine states *was evaluated*.

EXAMPLE: Net energy analyses *have been carried out* for eight trajectories which convert energy source into heated domestic water.

M   Methodology (past tense)

EXAMPLE: Children *performed* a 5-trial task.

R   Results (past tense)

EXAMPLE: Older workers *surpassed* younger ones in both speed and skill jobs.

C   Conclusions (present tense/tentative verbs/modal auxiliaries)

EXAMPLE: The results *suggest* that the presence of unique sets of industry factors *can be used* to explain variation in economic growth.

EXERCISE 9.6   Identification

Read the following abstract from a civil engineering study about a test of an experimental type of pavement construction. Underline each <u>present tense verb</u> once, each <u>past tense verb</u> twice, and draw a circle around any (modal auxiliaries) you find.

MODEL STUDY OF ANCHORED PAVEMENT

Abstract. [1]Roadways constructed of conventional pavement are subject to deformations after prolonged use. [2]A laboratory model study of an anchored pavement was carried out. [3]The objective of the study was to investigate construction problems and to develop specifications for a full-scale test. [4]The study compared 1/20-scale anchored pavement and conventional slabs of similar dimensions. [5]The model test results were compared with results from finite-element analysis. [6]The deformations were lower for the anchored pavement compared with those for the conventional slab, and stresses in the soil were reduced and distributed more widely by rigid anchors. [7]These findings indicate that an anchored slab offers distinct advantages over a conventional slab. [8]The ANSYS computer program could be used to analyze such a soil-structure system, incorporating the environmental and mechanical effects.

EXERCISE 9.7   Fill-in

The same abstract from the civil engineering report about pavement is given again here. This time, fill in each blank space with an appropriate verb or auxiliary. Do not look back at the original selection until you have finished.

MODEL STUDY OF ANCHORED PAVEMENT

[1]Roadways constructed of conventional pavement
_____ subject to deformations after prolonged use. [2]A

laboratory model study of an anchored pavement _____ carried out. **3**The objective of the study _____ to investigate construction problems and to develop specifications for a full-scale test. **4**The study _____ 1/20-scale anchored pavement and conventional slabs of similar dimensions. **5**The model test results were _____ with results from finite-element analysis. **6**The deformations _____ lower for the anchored pavement compared with those for the conventional slab, and stresses in the soil _____ reduced and distributed more widely by rigid anchors. **7**These findings indicate that an anchored slab _____ distinct advantages over a conventional slab. **8**The ANSYS computer program _____ be used to analyze such a soil-structure system, incorporating the environmental and mechanical effects.

EXERCISE 9.8   Reconstruction

Use each group of key words here to form a sentence based on the abstract about anchored pavement. The words in each group are in the correct order, but you will need to add other words and word endings in order to make complete, grammatical sentences. Do not look back at the previous exercises until you have finished.

---

1. roadways
   conventional payment
   subject
   deformations
   prolonged use

2. laboratory model study
   anchored pavement
   carry out

3. objective
   this study
   investigate construction problems
   develop specifications
   full-scale test

4. model test results
   compare
   results
   finite-element analysis

5. deformations
   lower
   anchored pavement
   compare with
   conventional slab

6. findings
   indicate
   anchored slab
   offer
   distinct advantages
   conventional slab

7. ANSYS computer
   program
   be use
   analyze
   such
   soil-structure system

EXERCISE 9.9   Library

Using the same abstract example that you found for Library Exercise 9.5, analyze each sentence and answer the following questions:

1. What verb tense is used in each sentence?
2. Explain the reason for each verb tense used.
3. Do the verb tenses used in your example agree with the conventions you have learned here? What differences did you find?
4. Are any modal auxiliaries or tentative verbs used in your examples? Does their use follow the conventions we have studied in this chapter?

INTEGRATION

EXERCISE 9.10   Guided Writing

Read the following shortened version of a report from the field of English language learning. In the left margin write a code letter for each sentence to indicate what kind of information it contains (B = background, P = principal activity/purpose, M = methodology/materials, R = results, and C = conclusion). Now answer the following questions:

1. Based on your coding and what you have learned about experimental research reports, is there any information in this report that you would reorder?
2. Is there any information that you would add?

Now write an abstract for the report. Do not copy directly from the report; use your own words to express the author's ideas. Limit your abstract to 100 words.

ENGLISH LANGUAGE ACQUISITION:
THE EFFECTS OF LIVING WITH AN AMERICAN FAMILY

This study investigated the degree of English language acquisition of 83 students who were living in English-speaking environments during their 14-week term of formal language study. The purpose of the investigation was to compare rate of English acquisition of these students with that of their classmates who were living in dormitories or apartment situations, usually in close proximity to other speakers of their first language.

Fathman (1976) studied different sorts of second language learning programs and found that, "...(students) making the most marked improvement were in settings where the use of English was encouraged and necessary for communication." (Fathman 1976: 433). Subjects of this study were living with American families—that is, their English was encouraged and was necessary for communication.

Additionally, "one of the most important factors (in language learning) is the attitude of the learner to the language and its speakers." (Spolsky 1969: 271). The fact that living in the American family was elected by the student at slightly higher cost than other housing situations would seem to suggest a positive attitude and motivation.

Hypotheses tested:

H_1: Mean of TOEFL scores of homestay students = Mean of TOEFL scores of non-homestay students.

H_2: Mean of classroom grades of homestay students = Mean of classroom grades of non-homestay students.

Materials and procedure: All students took Michigan A or Placement Tests before beginning English instruction. For purposes of pretest and later statistical analysis each of the 83 homestay students was paired with a non-homestay student who had an identical Michigan A or Placement score (± 2).

Results: At the end of the 14 weeks of intensive (22.5 hours per week) English study, all students received classroom grades in grammar, reading, composition and spoken English. Some took the TOEFL. In all instances scores of homestay students were higher.

Discussion: Language learners and teachers have long assumed that the best way to learn a second language was by living in an environment in which it is used. This study lends strong empirical support to this assumption.

What this study does not do is separate the integrative motivation factor which may have influenced students to choose to live with American families from the exposure factor operative during that stay with the families. Future studies need to develop instruments which can make the distinction.

EXERCISE 9.11 Writing Up Your Own Research

In writing the abstract to your own research report, follow the procedure you have learned in this chapter. Select important information from each of the major sections of your report. Remember that you can write a *reduced* abstract by eliminating and combining information elements. Do not copy sentences directly from the report. Synthesize the information in your major sections into clear, concise statements that will give your reader an accurate preview of the contents of your report. Your abstract should not exceed 200 words.

CHECKLIST FOR CHAPTER 9

Abstracts

INFORMATION

_____ Select and order information from previous sections of your report corresponding to elements *B, P, M, R*, and *C*.

_____ For reduced abstracts, eliminate *B* statements and combine statements containing *P* and *M* information.

LANGUAGE

_____ Use appropriate verb tenses, tentative verbs, and modal auxiliaries, depending on which section of the report the information comes from.

CREDITS

The authors wish to acknowledge the following researchers and publishers who generously released their materials for use in this book.

Chapter 1

Rohrbach, N., and Stewart, B.R. "Using Microcomputers in Teaching." *The Journal of the American Association of Teacher Educators in Agriculture*, Vol. 27, No. 4, 18–25, 1986.

Lipscomb, T., McAllister, H., and Bregman, N. "Bias in Eyewitness Accounts: The Effects of Question Format, Delay Interval, and Stimulus Presentation." *Journal of Psychology*, Vol. 119, No. 3, 207–212, 1985. Reprinted with permission of the Helen Dwight Reid Educational Foundation. Published by Heldref Publications, 4000 Albemarle St., N.W., Washington, D.C. 20016. Copyright © 1986.

Chapter 2

The four-stage model of the introduction is based on the work of John Swales, and originally appeared as "Aspects of Article Introductions." *Aston ESP Research Report No. 1*, University of Aston in Birmingham, 1981.

Reprinted with permission of authors and publisher from Shank, M.D., and Haywood, K.M. "Eye Movements while Viewing a Baseball Pitch." *Perceptual and Motor Skills*, 1987, 64, 1191–1197.

Hillman, W.S., and Culley, D.D., Jr. "The Uses of Duckweed in Waste-Water Treatment." *American Scientist*, Vol. 66, No. 1, 1978.

Ashton, G.D. "River Ice." *American Scientist*, Vol. 67, No. 39, 1979.

Sutherland, D.G. "The Transport and Sorting of Diamonds by Fluvial and Marine Processes." *Economic Geology*, Vol. 77, No. 7, 1982.

Morse, C. "College Yearbook Pictures: More Females Smile than Males." *Journal of Psychology*, Vol. 110, No. 1, 3–6, 1982. Reprinted with permission of the Helen Dwight Reid Educational Foundation. Published by Heldref Publications, 4000 Albemarle St., N.W., Washington, D.C. 20016. Copyright © 1982.

Davis, R., and Hull, M.L. "Design of Aluminum Bicycle Frames." *Journal of Mechanical Design*, Vol. 103. American Society of Mechanical Engineers, 1981.

Anderson, J.U., Stewart, A.E., and Gregory, P.C. "A Portable Rainfall Simulator and Runoff Sampler." *New Mexico State University Agricultural Experiment Station Research Report No. 143*, 1968.

Chapter 3

Santos, P.F., Depree, E., and Whitford, W.G. "Spatial Distribution of Litter and Microarthropods in a Chihuahuan Desert Ecosystem." With permission from *Journal of Arid Environments*, Vol. 1, No. 1, 41. Copyright 1978 by Academic Press Inc (London) Limited.

Natriello, G., and Dornbusch, S.M. "Providing Direction and Building Commitment: Teaching as Institutional Leadership." *Educational Research Quarterly*, Vol. 7, No. 3, 30–31, 1982.

Shorrocks, A.F. "The Measurement of Mobility." *Econometrica*, Vol. 46, No. 5, 1013, 1978.

Mitchell, W.H. "Subsurface Irrigation and Fertilization of Field Corn." *Delaware Agricultural Experiment Station Paper No. 893*, 1980.

Calvo, G.A. "On the Time Consistency of Optimal Policy in a Monetary Economy." *Econometrica*, Vol. 46, No. 6, 1978.

Hoskins, M. "Reassessment of Food Practices and Preferences of Some University Students. *New Mexico State University Agricultural Experiment Station Bulletin No. 640*, 1976.

Benson, G.P., and Weigel, D.G. "Ninth Grade Adjustment and Achievement as Related to Mobility." *Educational Research Quarterly*, Winter 1980–81.

Riding, R.J., and Vincent, D.J. T. "Listening Comprehension: The Effects of Sex, Age, Passage Structure, and Speech Rate." *Educational Review*, Vol. 32, No. 3, 1980. Acknowledgment is made to the editors of *Educational Review* for permission to reprint.

Miller, T., and Gressis, N. "Nonstationarity and Evaluation of Mutual Fund Performance." *Journal of Financial and Quantitative Analysis*, Vol. 15, No. 3, 1980.

Weissberg, R.C., and Stuve, M. "Differential Gain Rates in Intensive ESL Programs." Reprinted with permission from *System*, Vol. 7, No. 1. Copyright 1979, Pergamon Press, Ltd.

Chapter 4

Davis, J., Stasch, A., and Vastine, W. "Food-Buying Practices of Students' Wives at New Mexico State University." *New Mexico State University Agricultural Experiment Station Bulletin No. 547*, 1969.

Gabriel, S., and Baker, C. "Concepts of Business and Financial Risk." *American Journal of Agricultural Economics*, Vol. 62, No. 3, 1980.

Swanson, G.R., and Williamson, K.J. "Upgrading Lagoon Effluents with Rock Filters." *Journal of the Environmental Engineering Division*, December 1980. Copyright 1980, The American Society of Civil Engineers.

Danok, A.B., McCarl, B.A., and White, T.K. "Machinery Selection Modeling: Incorporation of Weather Variability." *American Journal of Agricultural Economics*, Vol. 62, No. 4, 1980.

Steele K., Battista, M., and Krockover, G. "The Effect of Microcomputer-Assisted Instruction on the Computer Literacy of Fifth Grade Students. *Journal of Educational Research*, Vol. 76, No. 5, 299, May/June

1983. Reprinted with permission of the Helen Dwight Reid Educational Foundation. Published by Heldref Publications, 4000 Albemarle Street, N.W., Washington, D.C. 20016. Copyright © 1983.

Gent, A.N. "Some Chemical Effects in Fatigue Cracking of Vulcanized Rubbers." *Journal of Applied Polymer Science*, Vol. 6, No. 23, 497, 1962.

Mathis, S. "Programmable Measurement for Use in an Educational Environment." Master's thesis, New Mexico State University, 1974.

Coren, S., and Porac, C. "Fifty Centuries of Right-Handedness: The Historical Record." *Science*, Vol. 198, 631–632. November 1977. Copyright 1977 by the AAAS.

Chapter 5

Carrow, E. "Auditory Comprehension of English by Monolingual and Bilingual Preschool Children." *Journal of Speech and Hearing Research*, Vol. 15, 407–409, 1972.

Nelson, R.A., Beck, T., and Steiger, D. "Ratio of Serum Urea to Serum Creatinine in Wild Black Bears." *Science*, Vol. 226, 841–842, November 16, 1984. Copyright 1984 by the AAAS.

Lawrence, M., Lamb, W.H., Lawrence, F., and Whitehead, R.G. "Maintenance Energy Cost of Pregnancy and Influence of Dietary Status in Rural Gambian Women." *The Lancet*, August 18, 1984.

Casagrande, L. "Stabilization of Soils by Means of Electro-Osmosis." *Journal of the Boston Society of Civil Engineers*, ·275, March, 1983.

O'Neil, R.S. "Subway Construction Costs: The Role of the Engineer." *Journal of the Construction Division*, ASCE, December, 1980.

Sotiropoulos, E., and Cavounidis, S. "Cut and Cover Construction on Unstable Slopes." *Journal of the Construction Division*, ASCE, December, 1980.

Trujillo, P.M., and Whitworth, J. W. "Weed Control in Chile Peppers at the Española Valley Branch Station." *New Mexico State University Agricultural Experiment Station Research Report No. 213*, 1971.

Stevens, T.H. "An Economic Analysis of Natural Gas Policy Alternatives." *New Mexico State University Agricultural Experiment Station Research Report No. R357*, 1978.

Maloney, W.F., and McFillen, J.M. "Valence of and Satisfaction with Job Outcomes." *Journal of Construction Engineering and Management*, ASCE, Vol. 111, No. 1, 53–54, March, 1985. With permission.

Chapter 6

Saulnier, B. "A See-Saw Dryer." *Sharing the Sun: Solar Technology in the Seventies*, 12–13. Copyright 1976, American Section of the International Solar Energy Society.

Anderson, J.U., Stewart, A.E., and Gregory, P.C. "A Portable Rainfall Simulator and Runoff Sampler." *New Mexico State University Agricultural Experiment Station Research Report No. 143*, 1968.

Weissberg, R.C., and Stuve, M. "Differential Gain Rates in Intensive ESL Programs." Reprinted with permission from *System*, Vol. 7, No. 1. Copyright 1979, Pergamon Press, Ltd.

Srivastava, S., Minore, J., Cheung, C.K., and Noble, W.J. Reduction of Aromatic Rings by 2-Propanol with Raney Nickle Catalysis. Reprinted in part with permission from *The Journal of Organic Chemistry*, Vol. 50, 386–398. Copyright 1985 American Chemical Society.

Mackenzie, F., Stoffyn, M., and Wollast, R. "Aluminum in Seawater: Control by Biological Activity." *Science*, Vol. 199, 680–682, February 10, 1978. Copyright 1978 by the AAAS.

Begleiter, H., Porjesz, B., Bihari, B., and Kissin, B. "Event-Related Brain Potentials in Boys at Risk for Alcoholism." *Science*, Vol. 225, 1493–1496, September 28, 1984. Copyright 1984 by the AAAS.

"Investigating the Linguistic Acceptability of Egyptian EFL Students," by G.R. Tucker and M. Sarofim, 1979, *TESOL Quarterly*, Vol. 13, No. 1, p. 31. Copyright 1979 by TESOL. Adapted by permission.

Alternative Energy Resources, El Paso, Texas. "Be Solar Smart." 1981.

Adapted from "Product Technology and the Consumer" by G. Franklin Montgomery. Illustration by Ilil Arbel. Copyright © 1977 by *Scientific American, Inc.* All rights reserved.

Maloney, W.F., and McFillen, J.M. "Valence of and Satisfaction with Job Outcomes." *Journal of Construction Engineering and Management*, ASCE, Vol. III, No. 1, 53–54, March, 1985. With permission.

Chapter 7

Rhodes, N., and Snow, M.A. "Foreign Language in the Elementary School: A Comparison of Achievement." *ERIC/CLL News Bulletin*, Vol. 7, No. 2, March, 1984.

Rapoport, J., Buchsbaum, M., Zahn, T., Weingartner, H., Ludlow, C., and Mikkelsen, E. "Dextroamphetamine: Cognitive and Behavioral Effects in Normal Prepubertal Boys." *Science*, Vol. 199, 560–562, February 3, 1978. Copyright 1978 by the AAAS.

Carranco, P.D., Hernandez, A., and Rivera, F. "Soil and Aquatic Fungi in a Waste-Stabilization Pond System of the State of Mexico, Mexico." *Water, Air and Soil Pollution*, Vol. 23, 252–254. Copyright © 1984 by D. Reidel Publishing Company. Reprinted by permission of Kluwer Academic Publishers.

Markland, M. Shannon, and Rice, D. "A Comparison of Hemispheric Preference between High Ability and Low Ability Elementary Children." *Educational Research Quarterly*, Fall, 1983.

Vandewiele, M. "Fears of Senegalese Secondary School Students." *Journal of Psychology*, Vol. 107, 281–287, 1981. Reprinted with permission of the Helen Dwight Reid Educational Foundation. Published by Heldref Publications, 4000 Albemarle St., N.W., Washington, D.C. 20016. Copyright © 1981.

Vianna, N., and Polan, A.K. "Incidence of Low Birth Weight Among Love Canal Residents." *Science*, Vol. 226, 1217–1219, December 7, 1984 by the AAAS.

Giniger, S., Dispenzieri, A., and Eisenberg, J. "Age, Experience and Performance on Speed and Skill Jobs in an Applied Setting." *Journal of Applied Psychology*, Vol. 68, No. 3, 472–473, 1983. Copyright 1983 by the American Psychological Association. Reprinted by permission of the publisher and author.

Quadens, O., and Green, H. "Eye Movements During Sleep in Weightlessness." *Science*, Vol. 225, 221–222, July 13, 1984. Copyright 1984 by the AAAS.

Chapter 8

Giniger, S., Dispenzieri, A., and Eisenberg, J. "Age, Experience and Performance on Speed and Skill Jobs in an Applied Setting. *Journal of Applied Psychology*, Vol. 68, No. 3, 472–473, 1983. Copyright 1983 by the American Psychological Association. Reprinted by permission of the publisher and author.

Thompson, K., Luthans, F., and Terpening, W. "The Effects of MBO on Performance and Satisfaction in a Public Sector Organization." *Journal of Management,* Vol. 7, No. 1, 53–68, 1981.

Eve, R.A., and Bromley, D.G. "Scholastic Dishonesty Among College Undergraduates." *Youth and Society*, Vol. 13, No. 1, 3–22, 1981. Copyright 1981 by Sage Publications, Inc. Reprinted by permission of Sage Publications, Inc.

Matthews, K., and Seigel, J. "Type A Behaviors by Children, Social Comparison, and Standards for Self-Evaluation." *Developmental Psychology*, Vol. 19, No. 1, 135–140, 1983. Copyright 1983 by the American Psychological Association. Reprinted by permission of the publisher and author.

Knapper, C.K., and Cropley, A.J. "Interpersonal Factors in Driving." *International Review of Applied Psychology*, Vol. 29, 415–438, 1980. Copyright 1980 by the International Association of Applied Psychology.

Miara, R., Musselman, J., Navarro, J., and Shneiderman, B. "Program Indentation and Comprehensibility." *Communications of the ACM*, Vol. 26, No. 11, 866–867, 1983.

Jimenez, E. "The Value of Squatter Dwellings in Developing Countries." *Economic Development and Cultural Change*, Vol. 30, No. 4, 751–752, 1982. Published by The University of Chicago Press. Copyright 1982 by The University of Chicago Press.

Rowland, V.T., and Nickols, S. "How Is the Time Spent?" *Journal of Extension*, Vol. 23, 13–16, Spring, 1985.

Chapter 9

Gould, J., Conti, J., and Hovanyecz, T. "Composing Letters with a Simulated Listening Typewriter." *Communications of the ACM*, Vol. 26, No. 4, 295–307, 1983.

Matthews, K., and Seigel, J. "Type A Behaviors by Children, Social Comparison, and Standards for Self-Evaluation. *Developmental Psychology,* Vol. 19, No. 1, 135–140, 1983. Copyright 1983 by the American Psychological Association. Reprinted by permission of the publisher and author.

Bates, H.L. "The Readability of Individual Income Tax Instruction Booklets in South Carolina and Other Southeastern States." *Business and Economic Review*, Vol. 25, No. 2, 8–11, November, 1978.

Miara, R., Musselman, J., Navarro, J., and Shneiderman, B. "Program Indentation and Comprehensibility." *Communications of the ACM*, Vol. 26, No. 11, 866–867, 1983.

Keinath, W.F., Jr. "The Decentralization of American Economic Life: An Income Evaluation." *Economic Geography*, Vol. 58, No. 4, 343–357, 1982.

Karlen, D., and Camp, C. "Row Spacing, Plant Population and Water Management Effects on Corn in the Atlantic Coastal Plain." Reproduced from *Agronomy Journal*, Vol. 77, No. 3, 393–398, May–June 1985, by permission of the American Society of Agronomy, Inc.

Saxena, S.K., and Milisopoulos, S.G. "Model Study of Anchored Pavement." *Transportation Research Record No. 814*, 55–62, 1981. By permission of Transportation Research Board, National Research Council, Washington, D.C.

Acree, G. "English Language Acquisition: The Effects of Living with an American Family." *TESOL Quarterly*, Vol. 14, No. 3, 388–389, 1980. Copyright 1980 by TESOL. Reprinted with permission.

INDEX